I0766759

PeriWrinkle – Smoothing out Perinatal Mood and Anxiety Disorders

A Therapist's Personal and Professional Perspective by Susie Molek, MSCP, LPC

Copyright Information

© 2019 Susie Molek. All rights reserved. This book may not be reproduced in whole or in part, in any form or by any means, electronic or mechanical, including photocopying, recording, or by any information storage and retrieval system now known or here-after invented, without written permission from the publisher.

First Edition.

Disclaimer

The content of this book is provided for general information only. It is not intended to, and does not, amount to advice which you should solely rely; it is not intended as a substitute for the medical advice of physicians. The reader should regularly consult a physician in matters relating to his/her health and particularly with respect to any symptoms that may require diagnosis or medical attention.

This book is not meant to be used as a replacement for individual counseling, group therapy, medical assessment, or any treatment. Please obtain relevant professional assistance if you are struggling with any issues. If you have questions about any medical matter, you should consult your doctor or other professional healthcare provider as soon as possible.

All stories are real from author's interviews. Some names have been changed or only include the first name or initials to protect the privacy of individuals.

Cover Photo

Photography: Rachel Lauren

Hair Stylist: Nicole Angotti

Models: Susie Molek

Logan from Ironwood Wolves

PeriWrinkle Outline

Part I – Information/Education

Page

About the Author: Susie Molek, MSCP, LPC

Born and raised in beautiful Garrett County, Maryland; transplanted to the wonderful city of Pittsburgh, Pennsylvania.

This particular story of my life began nine years ago. I was a birth doula and a therapist for postpartum depression at the time. I taught childbirth and parenting classes. I had a wealth of information at my fingertips. I had coping skills overflowing from my mental tool bag. The irony of it all…I, the therapist, was not immune. Postpartum anxiety and depression struck with an intimidating and forceful blow. I first fell over, then apart. I thought I would have to quit my job. But somehow, through the dark and through the difficult terrain, something magical happened. I struck back and surprised postpartum with the strength of my uppercut. I had a beautiful new baby to enjoy and I was determined to live again for me and for my child. Here is my story, both professional and personal, and the story of some other amazing and beautiful survivors. I have also included a section called "*Grow Me*" with some tips and positive vibes.

Currently, I am a Licensed Professional Counselor with a private practice. I received my Master of Science in Counseling Psychology from Chatham University in Pittsburgh and a B.A. degree in Psychology from Point Park University in Pittsburgh.

I work with women who experience perinatal mood and anxiety disorders, perinatal bereavement, fertility issues, and women with other stressors, depression, grief, and anxiety.

I am a mother of a beautiful nine year old daughter, Skyla. We live with our fur-babies, Summer - a Bengal cat (who sometimes frequents the office with me) and Skyla's pet ferret, Sprightly. My daughter and I love to travel, we love nature, animals, and adventure. In the summer, you will most likely find me on my Paddleboard on some body of water. Skyla is a very talented artist. I cannot draw a stick figure. I, on the other hand, am the writer. So, you might find us both with a pencil in one hand, but a journal in my other hand, and a sketchbook in hers.

I have happily and passionately added author and public speaker to my career accomplishments in recent years. In addition to this book, you can find *"Swimming in a Sea of Octopuses: Adapting to Increasing Speeds of Life,"* on Amazon.

I hope you find some or all of this book helpful. If you have happened upon this book for yourself or for a loved one, know that there is help, hope, and resources. I wish the best for you. You are here for a reason. You matter.

P.S. – Some of the chapters I tried to KISS – keep it short and sweet because of many reasons: it's a busy world; if you are already not feeling like yourself then your focus might not be as sharp; many of us are acclimated to a faster technological world with quick, scroll-worthy, snippets on social media; because I didn't want to bore myself either; and because I want this to be just a part of you getting/feeling better. Consider it a piece of your treatment network; not a whole, because what is really beneficial is a conglomeration of all the goodness you can receive: books, friends, family, therapists, doctors, medication, helplines, support groups, your own amazing self, etc.

Introduction

When I was writing this book, I noticed I was often interchanging terminology for the subject. I wanted one word that I could use throughout to signify mood and anxiety issues after birth. Most people just say "postpartum." Postpartum, however, can refer to anything post-birth including physical recovery. I wanted something specific to the emotional and mental health aspect. Around the world, it is the same, with different names:

PPD - Postpartum Depression

PND -Perinatal Depression

PMAD - Postpartum Mood and Anxiety Disorders

MMH – Maternal Mental Health

PANDA – Perinatal Anxiety and Depression Australia

PANDAS – Pre and Post Natal Depression Advice and Support

Just to name a few. These are all wonderful, but I needed ONE simple word.

The colloquial term I decided on: *PeriWrinkle* – of or around the wrinkle in time, a momentary space during pregnancy and after childbirth, where life isn't quite the same or as expected. Where there is light and dark. A place where I offer you courage and optimism to reign over the bad. Where positivity transpires and hope exists for all those afflicted. A place where PeriWrinkle will become periwinkle – which in Ukraine folklore, periwinkle is tied to love that lasts through eternity. That's the goal. Love, bonding, and attachment…mother and baby, for a lifetime.

This book will provide information on multiple perinatal mental health issues and smoothing out the wrinkles related to perinatal mood disorders. I have also included real life accounts from real life women who have experienced it and their partners who were either there to help, or perhaps experienced their own form of it. It is my story, it is the story of many women and men. In raising awareness and sharing our experiences, may we break the silence and begin diminishing the stigma. If children are the future, then why, why are we not taking better care of their caretakers?

I want to shift the focus. Postpartum Depression has been in the spotlight too long. It is time to share the limelight with the other perinatal mood disorders. We tend to focus mainly on depression after childbirth, however, anxiety tends to be more prevalent than ever. Not that depression isn't serious and important. It absolutely is, however, it is not the only issue afflicting mothers.

I want to iron out a few wrinkles here. Perinatal Mental Illness isn't just depression. In fact, more women might be experiencing anxiety during pregnancy and/or postpartum. Another wrinkle: "I don't want to hurt my baby, so I must not have postpartum." That statement leaves women saying they are fine, but not feeling fine. The incongruence equates to a lack of understanding on society's part in which postpartum is being limited to just severe cases of hospitalization, suicide and/or infanticide. This can lead to underdiagnoses and lack of proper treatment. We focus so much on that one wrinkle of depression, we neglect to see the other wrinkles in perinatal time that could be troubling our beautiful mommas. If we bring to life the rest of the struggles, increase awareness, and provide better screening, we can deliver better targeted treatment and more hope.

I want the colors of conception and delivery: the pinks, the blues, the yellow, the green, and purple to stay vibrant. Unfortunately, sometimes, all the color fades and turns dark. When the baby blues turn gray or even black…When it adds wrinkles to our weary, worn out moms…I want this book to be a positive light on a struggle so many woman are facing and have survived. May it add lively colors back into the beautiful mommas around the world! May it smooth out the wrinkles as you remember, this is only a PeriWrinkle in time!

Inspiration from a Specialist

Two years ago, I had the pleasure of meeting Doctor Sarah Homitsky at a workshop in 2017 on *Identifying and Treating Perinatal Mood and Anxiety Disorders.* Sarah Homitsky, MD is a pediatrician and psychiatrist with clinical expertise in the treatment of pregnancy-related mood and anxiety disorders. She graduated from Michigan State University College of Human Medicine and completed her triple board residency at the University of Pittsburgh Medical Center.

I knew from the moment I met her that she exuded passion for her work in providing integrated perinatal psychiatric services for women with behavioral health issues, including pregnancy and postpartum depression, anxiety, and mood disorders. A specialty that is much needed. She is a true gem, a ray of light, and breath of fresh air. Sometimes you just know when someone is meant to do the work they do. These are the vibes I get with Dr. Homitsky. She, as well as other staff members at West Penn, quickly became a frequent referral source for my counseling patients when needing additional care and/or medication management.

I spoke with Dr. Homitsky again on the phone, December 2018, and she invited me to come tour the new facility at West Penn Hospital for pregnancy-related depression and anxiety disorders. The center is made possible by a collaboration from Allegheny Health Network (AHN) and the Alexis Joy D'Achille Foundation. I was flattered and ecstatic. Just a few weeks after that conversation, I visited the 7,300-square-foot, $2.5 million facility includes rooms for individual therapy as well as space for Intensive Outpatient care, a three-hours-daily, three-days-a-week group therapy, child bonding and stress relief program. I discuss more of this tour and the inspiration behind it in Chapter 14.

When writing this book, I wanted some insight and a message of encouragement from a doctor, specifically in this field, for those experiencing perinatal mood disorders. Who better, than Dr. Homitsky? I was absolutely honored when she agreed to write a piece for this book. I tried fitting it in a later chapter, but I loved the uplifting, positive, and forward-thinking message so much, that it deserved a feature here in the beginning. Here is her powerful and uplifting statement:

Over the last three years, we have witnessed a rapid expansion of perinatal mental health services in the greater Pittsburgh area. Healthcare systems and their providers are more appreciative of the fact that countless women experience perinatal depression and anxiety, and recognize the importance of universal screening to improve the identification of these disorders, followed by rapid referral. Perinatal mental health specialists are more accessible and providers are building innovative mother-baby treatment centers allowing mothers the opportunity to get the mental health treatment they need without having to be separated from their newborn babies. Women are partners in their treatment alongside providers who listen to and value their opinions.

Healthy mothers are an integral part of healthy families and communities, and thus we must keep the momentum going. Let's continue to recommend radical changes to our healthcare system that support our mothers. Let's address barriers to care to increase our clinical reach and ensure every mother gets the care and support she needs. And let's applaud the strong women stepping forward, willing to share their personal struggles with perinatal depression and anxiety in an effort to decrease stigma and draw attention to these incredibly important health topics.

~Sarah Homitsky, MD

<u>Chapter 1: The Array of Postpartum Mental Health</u>

Baby Blues

Baby Pinks

Postpartum Depression

Postpartum Anxiety

Postpartum OCD (Obsessive Compulsive Disorder)

Postpartum Bipolar

Postpartum Psychosis

Postpartum PTSD (Post-Traumatic Stress Disorder)

Perinatal Issues with Autism

PPND – Paternal Postnatal Depression (Dads)

<u>Baby Blues</u>

Different from perinatal mood is a very common occurrence in women during the perinatal phase. A time after delivery and up to 14 days after in which women might experience what is known as the Baby Blues.

When I would tell my students in childbirth class that the Baby Blues affected about 80% of women, many of them looked a bit scared. This is not the same as postpartum and is quite normal considering all the hormonal fluctuations and the fact that you just birthed a real human being via your vagina or stomach. And now, you still have to figure out how to take care of said tiny human, while you put frozen pads in your own diaper, have to birth again your first bowel movement, and oh yeah, your boobs are on fire because nourishing, warm, amazing breast milk develops after colostrum and they are ready to explode with a showering storm of liquid gold.

You're allowed to feel a little off.

Typically the onset is within the first week postpartum and can last up to three weeks. It is not considered a disorder, but I mention it because of the high frequency of occurrence and to differentiate between postpartum depression and other mood disorders. Most new moms get the blues.

Symptoms of Baby Blues

- o Mood Instability
- o Sadness
- o Anxiety
- o Fatigue
- o Lack of Concentration
- o Feelings of Dependency
- o Sometimes crying for no apparent reason

Baby Pinks

Like Baby Blues, this is not a formal diagnosis or disorder. Consider it postpartum euphoria. Psychiatrist Ariel Dalfen, head of the perinatal mental health program at Toronto's Mount Sinai Hospital uses the clinical term – hypomania. In the UK, baby pinks are referred to as "the highs." This is sometimes a precursor to postpartum bipolar, but not always. It can also occur in women with an already existing diagnosis of bipolar.

Symptoms typically appear in the first few days after childbirth and women feel like they are on top of the world. Possibly more talkative than normal and needing less sleep. If it gets to the point where behaviors become odd, seek treatment.

Postpartum Depression: When Baby Blues turn Gray

As discussed earlier, Baby Blues occurs in approximately 80% of mothers. Postpartum Depression occurs in about 15-20% of mothers. The onset is usually gradual, or sometimes rapid, within the first year after birth.

Symptoms Can Include:

Symptoms vary from person to person. It's unlikely that one person will experience all of them, but symptoms can include:

- Irritability or anger
- Anxiety
- Mood swings
- Excessive worrying
- Fears/Phobias
- Sleep problems, such as insomnia or excessive sleep
- Appetite changes

- Suicidal thoughts
- Lack of interest in the baby and/or discomfort around baby
- Lack of interest in things once enjoyed
- Feeling disconnected from the baby
- Thoughts of harming the baby
- Sluggishness
- Exhaustion
- Memory loss
- Sense of guilt or shame
- Sense of doom
- Hopelessness
- Scary or odd thoughts that repeat in your mind
- Low Self-Esteem
- Low Sex Drive
- Inability to focus
- Physical Symptoms/Complaints without apparent cause

Postpartum Anxiety/Panic Disorder

Anxiety is considered to be more common than postpartum depression, but it is rarely talked about or incorporated into childbirth education courses. Perinatal

Panic disorder occurs in about 10% of mothers and is more extreme than your average momma bear worries.

Postpartum Panic occurs in about 10% of women.

<u>Symptoms Can Include:</u>

Extreme Anxiety
Physical symptoms such as shaking or trembling
Shortness of breath, chest pain/tightness
Feeling dizzy, lightheaded, disoriented
Restlessness, Irritability, Agitation, Feeling on Edge
Hot or cold flashes, feeling flush, numbness, tingling
Sensation of racing heart, skip a beat, pounding heart
Chills, sweating
Nausea, stomach issues
Fear of dying or going crazy
Feeling like you've lost control
Sometimes awakened by these symptoms at night
Tense Muscles
Choking Sensation
Urge to flee
Feeling like you're crawling out of your skin

Postpartum OCD (Obsessive Compulsive Disorder)

Some people don't believe me when I say this is a thing, but it's definitely a thing. We just don't talk enough about maternal mental health enough or it just all gets lumped together as Postpartum Depression.

OCD develops in about 3-5% of new moms. More on the rare end, but it does and can occur.

Symptoms Can Include:

- o Intrusive, repetitive, persistent thoughts.
- o Intrusive, repetitive, persistent mental images.
- o Thoughts often are about hurting or killing the baby and a sense of horror over these thoughts.
- o Terrifying automatic, unwelcomed thoughts.
- o Thoughts cause distress in the mom.
- o Compulsions/actions to reduce the anxiety around that thought such as locking windows, hiding knives, not starting the fireplace, etc…
- o Perfectionism
- o Rituals, checking, seeking reassurance, and or avoiding feared situations.

"There is no reported case of a mum acting on her obsessional intrusive thoughts." (maternalocd.org)

- ➤ The negative thoughts are more terrifying for women than anything else.
- ➤ The obsessions are the unwanted thoughts and images.
  - o "What if I dropped the baby?"

> o "What if I didn't clean enough and contaminated the baby?"
- ➤ The compulsions are the rituals created to suppress the distress and/or prevent feared outcome.

Postpartum Bipolar

The rates in which this occurs is unclear and often misdiagnosed as something else like depression. Bipolar disorder fluctuates between different levels of mania to depression and cycles back again with varied rates of time in between.

Symptoms Can Include:

- Mania
    - o Hypomania – more mild version of mania
    - o Full blown
    - o Increased energy and activity
    - o Irritability
    - o Risk taking behaviors
    - o Increased spending
    - o Reckless behavior
    - o Increased sex drive
    - o Racing thoughts
    - o Rapid speech
    - o Decreased sleep or does not feel the need for sleep
    - o Grandiose Ideas
    - o Hallucinations, Delusions
- Depression
- Rapid and Severe Mood Swings

Postpartum Psychosis

This is a rare illness especially in comparison to postpartum depression and anxiety. Rare, but the most severe form of any postpartum psychiatric illness. It occurs in 1 to 2 of every 1000 women with a 5% suicide rate and a 4% infanticide rate. The onset is usually sudden and severe and typically within the first 2 weeks postpartum. The most significant risk factors for postpartum psychosis are a personal or family history of bipolar disorder, or a previous psychotic episode.

There is speculation that it is most likely underreported as some women suffer in silence, too afraid to tell anyone. Yet it can be preventable. It is treatable. There is help. Help for postpartum psychosis requires psychiatric evaluation and most likely hospitalization as the woman is out of touch with reality. Therapy alone is not effective for psychosis. In a psychotic state, some of her delusions or beliefs make sense to her even if they wouldn't any other day. She may be convinced there is a need to kill her baby or hear violent commands. This is why it is imperative to seek immediate treatment. Not all women will experience thoughts of harm or experience violent commands. Delusions are not always destructive, but there is always risk of danger when someone is in a delusional state with possibility of irrational judgement and potential impulsivity.

Symptoms Can Include:

- o Hallucinations – visual and/or auditory

- o Delusional thinking – false beliefs
- o Strange Beliefs
- o Paranoia and suspiciousness
- o Difficulty communicating at times
- o Feeling very irritated
- o Delirium-like appearance
- o Confusion, derealization, depersonalization, disorientation
- o Out of touch with reality
- o Lack of Insight – usually others notice her behavior is different
- o Mania

PTSD – Post-Traumatic Stress Disorder

Contrary to popular belief, war soldiers are not the only ones who experience PTSD. Although commonly linked to war, it is not exclusive to the military. The concept is the similar having experienced and/or witnessed a distressing event/situation. Many people may experience PTSD, including new moms. In fact, it occurs in up to 6% of women.

The risks – past traumatic events and most often it is caused by real or perceived trauma during vaginal or cesarean birth. Trauma being the distinguishing factor between this and postpartum depression.

Examples of Birth Trauma include:

- o Cord Prolapse

- o Use of vacuum extractor or forceps to deliver baby
- o Unplanned C-section
- o Emergency C-section
- o Severe complications for mom such as postpartum hemorrhage, severe 3rd or 4th degree perineal tearing, etc.
- o Infant needing to go to NICU (Neonatal Intensive Care Unit)
- o Feeling unheard, unimportant, and powerless during delivery
- o Previous rape or sexual abuse in which the birth experience is a trigger

- **<u>Symptoms Can Include:</u>**
  - o Recurrent Nightmares
  - o Flashbacks
  - o Extreme Anxiety
  - o Feelings of detachment, depersonalization
  - o Reliving past traumatic events
    - Physical or Emotional
    - Sexual
    - Childbirth trauma
    - Other difficult life events
  - o Hypervigilance
  - o Exaggerated startle response
  - o Wanting to avoid hospital where delivered baby

PeriWrinkle on the Spectrum – Pregnancy and Postpartum with Autism

I just wanted to mention this briefly as I have not heard it discussed a whole lot, however it is a part of our world. If you have autism or know someone who has it, this is for you.

Growing up, an '80s baby, I never heard the word Autism. However, it existed and some of the people who went undiagnosed have had children and are having children today. I think as more research arises and we have more people diagnosed with autism (not so many unknowns), we can now have open and honest conversations about what it means to have autism and start a family. Of course, remembering that autism is on a spectrum and there are varying ranges of symptoms and functionality, so there can never be a one size fits all. I have met some women with autism who have no desire to have children, some in which it never even crosses their mind really, some who have babies and struggle and rely on support from their partner and families, and I know some who are successful mothers. There are too many factors to know and predict every situation. If you have autism and want a family, keep in touch with your doctor to help you reflect and discuss what it might be like and if it is right for you.

Pregnancy with Autism

If this is you, know that pregnancy and the postpartum period might be a bit difficult for you too and in some different ways. For example, if you struggle with sensory issues, you may notice more of the changes and be sensitive to them. Sense of smell can be heightened in pregnancy and possibly more sensitive if you have autism. Some women report a greater sense of interoception – more awareness of what's going on inside your body.

As for labor and delivery – having been a doula myself for many years, I recommend a doula for you. I say this because you will not have a nurse with you every minute so it is just nice to have someone there to help you with the entire process, to know what it happening, what to expect next, etc. Even if you don't like touch and don't want a massage or anything in labor, a doula can help suggest positions, be moral support, help you communicate with staff, and so much more. Just an idea. It might also be quite an adjustment for you once baby arrives. A postpartum doula may help as well. If you like structure and routine, anticipate that it will be thrown off for a while and you will be operating on baby's timeframe until a schedule can be adapted.

It is good to recognize potential struggles and prepare in advance. Seek support from your medical team and loved ones. For example, if eye contact is difficult for you, talk to your doctor about other ways and having your partner help to make sure bonding and attachment is occurring.

There are some people with autism who may never have children and some are perfectly fine with that. I have heard this question before: "Can a woman with autism be a good mom?" Of course. Some make incredible moms because they are going that extra mile to research, research, research then learn all the best ways to do everything right. Some might be a bit too perfectionistic when it comes to motherhood that they might just have to cut themselves some slack sometimes, give themselves a fist bump for all their hard work, and remember to relax too.

Maybe you were not even diagnosed until your child's diagnosis and this is all new to you. Your story may help others. Every person is different. Every situation is different. Every pregnancy is different. Every child is different. It all just depends. I still think more research is needed on this topic. Also, more research in a positive light.

Know yourself. Know your limits. Keep in touch with your supports.

<u>Book Suggestion:</u>

"From Here to Maternity: Pregnancy and Motherhood on the Autism Spectrum" by Lana Grant.

<u>Dads</u>

Hey there men. You are not forgotten. PeriWrinkle is systemic, affecting the whole family.

You are often the main person supporting your wife and helping take care of your child. A life changing event. Men can get what is known as PPND – Paternal Postnatal Depression. A serious condition experienced by about 10% of men that without effective treatment, can result in damaging, long-term consequences for you, your child, and your entire family. There is hope. With proper treatment and support, men can fully recover from this depression. You will get through this too.

"The fact is, one in four new dads in the United States become depressed – which amounts to 3,000 dads who become depressed each day. It's normal for dads to need help as they enter fatherhood," says Will Courtenay, PhD, LCSW. (Rosen & Kelly, 2018).

If you are feeling overwhelmed, sad, hopeless, insecure, angry, irritable, easily frustrated, or experiencing your own fears and worries, seek help for yourself. Talk to others who have experienced and survived postpartum dadhood. Spend time with your baby and trust in your own abilities to be an amazing parent.

Both moms and dads have so many amazing things to offer baby and both are deserving of feeling good while raising their children. Please don't feel like you have to suffer alone or stuff it all in to be strong for everyone else. This can backfire and lead to worsening symptoms. Below are some resources to help you get back to you too.

Some resources just for dads:

Websites:

postpartumdads.org

postpartummen.com

Book:

The Postpartum Husband by Karen Kleiman

<u>A Final Note – ADHD/ADD (Attention Deficit Hyperactivity Disorder)</u>

Just wanted to quickly mention this as it is not something that just appears after birth, it is something you typically already have. If you have adult ADHD/ADD, know that sometimes symptoms can be exacerbated after giving birth especially with the sudden drop in hormone levels. When estrogen decreases, so can dopamine. If labor and postnatal hormone fluctuations are messing with your serotonin and dopamine, you might be feeling the impacts. Talk with your doctor and take care of you as it can make your previous symptoms increase and/or feel more overwhelming. Adapting to the extra stimuli with a newborn baby is not always easy for someone who has ADHD. The extra responsibilities, the extra stimulus, harder to balance everything, feeling more disorganized, feeling overwhelmed, possible criticism from others who do not "get it" or understand, etc. Give yourself some down time to recharge when you need. Find outside help if it would be helpful and alleviate some stress.

<u>Chapter 2: Pregnancy</u>

I was so excited to be pregnant. Ready and waiting for that alien ship to beam down light right on me…#glowing! Then all these not so glowing things happened. Morning, all-day and all night sickness happened. Round ligament pain. Chin acne. Fatigue worse than mono. Constipation. And what was that other thing…I forget…oh wait…Pregnancy brain. Yep. Seriously so glowing, but couldn't remember if I was or not.

But, really, despite the physical ailments, I was still excited and happy. I wanted so badly to be a mother. I couldn't wait for labor either. I had been a doula. It was time for my own birth my way.

For some women, depression and/or anxiety might begin even here during pregnancy. If you feel like your symptoms are more intense, hormonal fluctuations are throwing you off, if you start feeling too low and dreary and hopeless, if your self-esteem is plummeting, you don't enjoy things like you used to, and just don't feel like doing much including eating…You might be experiencing depression during pregnancy.

It is important to receive intervention as soon as possible as depression during pregnancy has been associated with preterm deliveries, low birth weight, and decreased bonding. Increased anxiety during pregnancy also means increased stress hormones like cortisol levels. We know that everything goes straight to baby via the placenta, including cortisol.

There are medications that are considered acceptable and safe during pregnancy. Reach out and find a good doc who is savvy with pregnancy and postpartum, up to date on the newest research, and can help connect you to medication and/or a therapist to help you. If you are experiencing it during pregnancy, it is more likely that it will continue and/or worsen after delivery. It is better to find a professional who can help you and can discuss risk verses benefit.

Chapter 3: Why?

Why is this so important? Perinatal Mood and Anxiety Disorders are the number one complication related to childbearing. There are tragic consequences ranging from relationship issues, divorce, unemployment, child neglect and abuse, developmental delays and behavioral problems, to death including: infanticide, homicide, and suicide.

It is a detectable illness. Assessment tools exist. Self-report. Family and friends noticing differences. Doctors like Ob-Gyns and Pediatricians can and should screen.

With more than 400,000 infants born to mothers who are depressed, perinatal depression is the most underdiagnosed obstetric complication in the United States (Bass & Bauer).

When left untreated, perinatal mood and anxiety disorders can have profound adverse effects on women and their children, ranging from increased risk of poor adherence to medical care, exacerbation of medical conditions, loss of interpersonal and financial resources, smoking and substance use, suicide, and infanticide. Perinatal mood and anxiety disorders are associated with increased risks of maternal and infant mortality and morbidity and are recognized as a significant patient safety issue. (ACOG Consensus Bundle on Maternal Health).

<u>Chapter 4: The Ultimate Tragedy – Suicide</u>

"Get over it. You'll be fine. Women have been having babies since the beginning of time. What's the worst that could happen?"…Suicide. That's what could happen. It is one of the leading causes of maternal death.

One in Seven women have depression in the year after they give birth according to a study released in the online edition of JAMA Psychiatry on March 13, 2018. One in five of the women had thoughts of harming themselves. Twenty percent of the studied group was diagnosed with bipolar disorder which can be worsened by antidepressant drugs. (Rope, 2018). Suicide accounts for about 20 percent of postpartum deaths – the second leading cause of death for women in the postpartum period. The United States has one of the worst rates, 1 in 5 postpartum deaths are suicide related. (Costello, 2018).

Grigoriadis and colleagues recently published a study having used a retrospective, population-based cohort to explore rates of suicide in women during pregnancy and the first postpartum year. An excellent aspect of this study was expanding the definition of perinatal suicide to include the entire first year postpartum, not just the first six weeks. In a 15 year period, they found that suicide accounted for 5.3% (51 of 966) of perinatal deaths. Approximately 1 out of every 19 deaths in pregnant or postpartum women. I have to stop to absorb and process this heartache for a moment. (Zagrabbe, 2018).

According to the study, perinatal women most frequently completed suicide at 9 – 12 months postpartum. (Grigoriadis et al., 2017). If you have any thoughts of harm, please reach out to someone, now. If someone you love is talking about it or saying things like they think their baby would be better off without them. She needs support from professionals right away. Our mommas are too important to not take it seriously.

When I attended a PSI (Postpartum Support International) Conference in Philadelphia in 2017, I was able to see two memory quilts up close and personal with the names of women who died by suicide because of a postpartum mood disorder. I can't even begin to describe the chill bumps it gave me to see and stand in front of those quilts of beautiful souls. The tears that formed in my heart. I took a quiet moment. Honoring those names. A part of me thinking, "That could have been me. That could have been anyone I know. Those are all someone's loved one." Written words of names that were once beautiful lives here on earth. The solemn sadness that overcame me was overwhelming at first and somehow was followed by the gratitude and love, to honor them, to pay it forward and make their lives a blessing and help save others. By their legacy and testament to help other women. For people like me and you who can help make an impact and save beautiful mommas from the grips of a devastating disorder. I hope to see less names on these quilts and more names on survival stories. *You are a gift to this world. I want to see the light in you shine here on earth. Someday you might be the hope for someone else.*

<u>Chapter 5: Causes and Risk Factors</u>

Everyone is vulnerable.

There is definitely no one easy reason or pinpoint item to explain why and sometimes it is a multitude of factors that create a perfect storm. From hormones, neurochemistry, current events, life history, and beyond.

The American College of Obstetricians and Gynecologists says that hormones, emotional factors, fatigue and general life stressors can all play a major role in the possibility of developing postpartum mental health issues. "After giving birth, hormone concentrations drop by 100 fold within a matter of days," says Katherine Wisner, MD. A sudden disruption like this in hormone levels may create disturbances in mood. There is also research suggesting that both pre-gestational and gestational diabetes may increase the risk of the condition.

Cheryl Beck has created the Postpartum Depression Predictors Inventory, a list of 13 variables that may be used to identify women at risk for postpartum depression either during pregnancy or soon after delivery (Beck, 2001).

- Prenatal depression – Depression during pregnancy may be the strongest predictor for later suffering from PPD.
- Prenatal anxiety
- History of previous depression – Although not as strong a predictor as a depressive episode during the pregnancy, it appears that women with histories of

depression previous to conception are also at a higher risk of PPD than those without.
- Maternity blues – Especially when severe, the blues may herald the onset of PPD.
- Recent stressful life events
- Inadequate social supports
- Poor marital relationship – One of the most consistent findings is that among women who report marital dissatisfaction and/or inadequate social supports, postpartum depressive illness is more common.
- Low self-esteem
- Childcare stress
- Difficult infant temperament

In addition, three factors are less definitively predictive, but still arise consistently as factors that increase a woman's risk of PPD, especially in combination with one or more of the factors listed above:

- Single marital status
- Unplanned or unwanted pregnancy
- Lower socioeconomic status

And to add/reiterate some indicators of increased risk:

- Financial hardships
- Previous History
- Lack of social support
- Social Isolation
- Societal Pressures
- Super Mom Syndrome

- Overworked, overwhelmed and without a village in modern times.
- Abrupt weaning
- History of PMS (premenstrual syndrome) or PMDD (premenstrual dysphoric disorder).
- Thyroid dysfunction
- Nutritional deficiencies
- Sensitivities to birth control or fertility medications
- Difficult childbirth or one that didn't go as expected. Such as unanticipated cesarean section.
- Family history of mood and/or anxiety disorders
- Genetics
- Hormones, Hormones, Hormones
- Any Gender – PeriWrinkle doesn't discriminate
- Family History
- Younger moms
- Stress of having new baby
- Poor Diet
- Difficult infant temperament
- Incongruence between expectations and reality of motherhood

Did you know? 1 in 7 Moms and 1 in 10 Dads suffer from postpartum depression. (PSI)

<u>Chapter 6: Impact on Infant</u>

When it comes to PeriWrinkle, it is not restricted to mom. When a mother is impacted, unfortunately babies can be the victims and experience some effects.

<u>Effects on Baby of Untreated Perinatal Mood Disorders</u>

- Infant can become withdrawn, irritable, and inconsolable
- Display insecure attachment
- Developmental Problems: cognitive, social, emotional, behavioral
- Higher risks of anxiety disorders and depression in childhood and adolescence
- If mom has increased levels of anxiety and stress = increased cortisol in baby too and more inconsolable
- Cortisol (stress hormones raging in mom's body) – stress activation of fight, flight reflex in infancy – as infant gets older, possible ADD (Attention Deficit Disorder) as a result
- More difficulties with breastfeeding
- Decreased Cognitive Performance
- Less creative play
- Poor development of self-regulation
- Helicopter Mom – highly anxious, a lot of "No" can be worse for bonding.
- Overcompensation by mom if she feels guilt over having postpartum mental health and she is overbearing and/or depletes her resources and

becomes tired, less present, and less in tune to baby's needs and cues.

- As an adolescent, potential anxiety, panic disorders, depression, conduct disorder, substance abuse, alcohol dependency
- Tension in the parent-child relationship
- Low Self-Esteem
- Infanticide. A tragic effect of postpartum psychosis. It is often not abusive – it is because mom is ill. It is not about being angry, it is about being delusional. It is a sad reality sometimes which is why early treatment is so essential.

<u>Healthy Bonding and Attachment</u>

Attachment is the emotional connection that babies form with caregivers based on shared experiences over a period of time that supports their social and emotional development throughout life.

This is difficult to achieve if mom is depressed and withdrawn. Eye contact and snuggles are important, but hard when a mom is not feeling herself. Try anyway. Get the help you need for you and your baby. Here are some ways to bond.

- ❖ Respond to cries. You cannot spoil a baby. Babies are tiny, sweet, floppy human beings who cannot do for themselves so they rely on us to help them when they are hungry, tired, wet, upset, etc. They learn to trust their adult humans when we respond to their needs. They feel safer and loved. Know that you will not and cannot be perfect and respond immediately all the time to every cry. You might be next up in the check-out line at the grocery store when baby starts crying. Please don't put baby on the conveyor belt with the rest of the food to change his/her diaper. It can wait until you check out or get to the car. Joking aside though, be careful that perfectionism does not try to rear its ugly head in the bonding and attachment department.

- ❖ Quality is more important than quantity. You do not need to be with your baby all the time. It is okay to take breaks. In fact, it is essential for your well-being. It is also good for baby to experience other people and social aspects.
- ❖ Try spending an hour a day looking into baby's eyes, encouraging laughter, and playing. Look into baby's eyes during feeding. Remember, an infant does not exit the womb pre-enlisted to Harvard. You do not need to try and reach every developmental milestone right away or push too hard or spend entire days working on reading and tummy time and vocabulary. Just think of that long-term student loan bill? They are babies not college students. ;)
- ❖ Self-Care. I cannot reiterate this enough. Take care of you so you have the energy and well-being to take care of baby too.
- ❖ Get support and ask for help if you need it.
- ❖ Skin-to-skin contact, especially in those early days. Even dads can do "kangaroo care" and hold baby to their bare chest.

- ❖ Infant massage. Relaxation and positive touch.
- ❖ Infant Stimulation –increase baby's attention span, curiosity, and memory by helping them explore the world with all five senses.
- ❖ Put your phone down and be present.
- ❖ Look into the mirror together. Make silly faces. Smile.
- ❖ Hugs and Kisses.
- ❖ Read to baby.
- ❖ Sing to baby.
- ❖ Narrate what you are doing. I loved walking Skyla around and engaging in one-way discourse with her. It is a great way to connect and help them develop vocabulary. And it is the cutest when they learn to engage and talk back with you.
  - "Look at this beautiful rose outside. It is a red flower with green leaves. Do you want to smell it with mommy?"
  - "Mommy is packing your diaper bag. Let's put bear in here. One, two, three diapers. One burp cloth …"
- ❖ Savor each moment as they grow. They might not do much and will not be very interactive early on. Delight in those newborn snuggles and then when they are responsive, enjoy play and laughter. As they grow more, you can enjoy more active moments.

<u>Side Note:</u> Just because you have a perinatal mood and/or anxiety disorder, doesn't mean you are not good with or bonding well with your baby. Despite perinatal mental health struggles, some moms are really great with baby and bonding. It is everything else that is wrong or difficult or stressful and she struggles more internally and in the moments she puts baby down for a nap or when others help, for example.

Chapter 7: Breastfeeding

A song to get stuck in your head. You're welcome.

"Let's talk about breast baby.

Let's talk about you and … baby."

My take on Breast verses Bottle.

Your body. Your Baby. Your decision.

Do I believe that breast is best? Of course human milk is best food for tiny human being. I believe that breast feeding is absolutely amazing and the benefits by far outweigh the competitor's (formula), but I do not believe it is the only way, the right way, and definitely NOT the "you're a bad mom if you don't" way – no way. It is not one correct answer. It's "D" – all of the above answer.

Exclusively BreastFeed! I am struggling with this and I worked places that pushed this. When we encourage this and a mom is unable to, even if she strongly desired to breastfeed but for some reason cannot– this is a set up for disappointment. A feeling of failure. Like her own body has failed her. It's an awful feeling.

It is being embedded and drilled into mom's heads that breastfeeding is the ONLY way. They begin to feel like a bad mother if for some reason they are unable to breast feed or due to a medical condition or the infant's intolerance. I have watched too women cry in distress to promote solely breast feeding. And I think it is important not to lead them on that it is easy and in the lovely video, the newborn baby crawls from mom's stomach up to her bosom and feeds naturally. Okay, if that happens to you, great. Awesome. I am really so happy for you, as this wasn't the case for me at all. I would never want other women to struggle. Most often it is more complicated than that.

Mom shame – the struggle is real. May we encourage, uplift and empower our beautiful mommas? Please! They are magical, sparkling beings who just delivered beautiful gifts into this world and now they have the capability to nourish their baby via whatever nipple they so desire. Their own nip, nips on nips (nipple shields), or a bionic replica (nipple on a bottle). Babies thriving = #goals. Extreme mom guilt = #notgoals.

There are also the highly anxious moms. "Am I doing okay? Producing enough milk?" The moms that don't even believe professionals when you prove with growth charts. Yes, moms worry, but when the degree of worry increases, this can be a sign of perinatal anxiety.

If you are a professional reading this book, I encourage you, stressful day or not, be encouraging and supportive. This can be a tough time for women and they need our love just as much as babies do.

I remember a nurse - I won't say her name, but I have never forgotten how she made me feel. And what she didn't know – what I did for a living. I had a breast reduction when I was 21. I still wanted to breastfeed and was pumped up about trying. She was to come for a home visit the first day after delivery (since I did not stay overnight at the midwife center). She came and made me feel awful that there was no way my baby was going to thrive if I was trying to breastfeed after the surgery I had and that already, I wasn't producing enough. But I teach childbirth. I help other women with breastfeeding issues. I only have colostrum right now. Baby has a marble sized belly. Despite what I knew, I let her get to me and let her stay too long inside my head. It was devastating. I now felt like a horrible mother. I should have called the center and told them. I wasn't thinking in the moment how maybe I could have helped save another mother from this treatment. I was too upset and down from hormonal changes and from her treatment, so that wasn't a thought. It needs to be said that staff members caring for our beautiful mothers, must provide best care and not do more harm. I should have said something. I hope you don't encounter this, but if you do, I encourage you to say something and if you don't have the energy to at that point, ask one of your support people to say something. It definitely added a wrinkle in my time of PeriWrinkle.

One last point. I also just want to raise awareness that when women stop breastfeeding they experience another crash in hormones. Some women are sensitive to this others are not. Just knowing that it could potentially cause mood to plummet can help reduce the shock value and allow you to prepare yourself in case. Some women are thrown off by this as they don't realize it could happen and begin to question everything. Family – take note and keep an eye on her during this time. Maybe she isn't just moody and you find that irritating. Be patient and kind and think, "Oh ya, she did stop breastfeeding. Her poor hormones are probably out of whack again."

Medication and Breast Feeding.

Talk to your doc. You might still be able to breast feed. If mom is taking meds during pregnancy – baby is already exposed to higher amount than what will be in the breast milk. Risk verses benefit. Don't give up hope on breast feeding if it is something you really wanted because you are taking or are considering taking medications to help with postpartum depression/anxiety. Find a doctor who can help you navigate this process. Especially one well versed in lactation pharmacology.

Research shows that moms with depression who are on medication, breastfed for longer durations than moms with untreated depression. "Many mothers could easily continue to breastfeed and take medication without risk to the infant." (Hale, 2019).

There might only be a trace that gets transferred to breast milk and even after that, oral bioavailability of the medication to the infant is considered. Many medications are destroyed or even fail to be absorbed by the infant's gut wall. "Drugs normally enter milk by passive diffusion driven by equilibrium forces between the maternal plasma compartment and the maternal milk compartment." (Hale, 2019). Some medications don't even make it from mom's liver to mom's plasma – the most important determinant when it comes to drug penetration. (Hale, 2019).

Some moms will resort to herbal supplements because they think this is healthier and better, but this can be risky with chemical substances that can be dangerous to infant. There are drugs with published, recent data for the treatment of perinatal mental issues and better ones with short half-lives. Again, best to seek good medical treatment and advice when it comes to medications while breastfeeding (including supplements and vitamins). Discussions for you and your doctor.

Chapter 8: Perinatal Loss and Bereavement

This topic is near and dear to my heart and deserves mention in this book. Perinatal loss is something that no parent ever wishes to encounter. It can include losses such as: miscarriage, ectopic pregnancy, molar pregnancy, stillbirth, neonatal death, and/or SIDS – Sudden Infant Death Syndrome.

I had the wonderful opportunity for many years to facilitate the Hugs for Healing Hearts program at St. Clair Hospital in Pittsburgh for pregnancy and infant loss as well as subsequent pregnancy after loss; running groups and hosting the memorial walks and holiday memorial service. I met so many beautiful women and families during that time and am honored they allowed me to be a small part of their big journeys.

Most likely, a woman you know has suffered a pregnancy related loss, whether you know it or not. Perhaps you, the reader, have had one or multiple losses.

Perinatal loss robs you of your hopes and dreams of your life with baby and you are left without the sweet bundle of joy you envisioned the moment you got pregnant. Even if you never saw your baby, you may have already started developing a bond the moment you knew you were pregnant with a beautiful life growing inside you; started imagining what life would be like with your baby. You may have thought about how you would care for your baby, maybe you even thought about what they might be when baby grows up. It can be an instant love like no other and when that suddenly and unexpectedly comes to a halt, the pain can be unimaginable.

If it was your first pregnancy, you were probably filled with anticipation of being a parent for the first time and what all that would entail. Partners are filled with joy. Dads looking forward to fatherhood – their dreams too are shattered in one tragic moment. Where does one begin when their world is suddenly uprooted? First, it's important that you give yourself permission to grieve. Know that it is not your fault. The various and overwhelming emotions are normal. You may feel: shock, confusion, disappointment, anger, guilt, self-blame, jealousy, frustration, sadness/depression, and maybe even experience physical symptoms. What you are going through is normal and everyone has their right to experience it and grieve in their own individual way.

Whether you were 4 or 40 weeks along, or momentarily held your baby in your arms, this was your baby who did exist. You might be making decisions you never imagined. Taking photos with your baby (I highly recommend). Planning an infant funeral. The cruel reminder of breast milk coming in, yet no baby there to feed. It is a lot to go through. Too many parents suffer in silence or solitude and feel that there is no appropriate way for them to talk about their grief. And yet, these experiences are not uncommon and do not happen in isolation.

If you have experienced a loss and later become pregnant again, the innocence of pregnancy is most often replaced with anxiety. It can be overwhelming and no one can take away that worry from you. I encourage you to try not to let it consume you though. Perhaps plan some activities to look forward to throughout the pregnancy to give your mind some nice distractions like maybe a day at the zoo, a date night with your partner, try a new hobby like painting or quilting, taste test new restaurants, etc.

<u>Supporters</u>

For family and friends wanting to support. Sometimes you may not know what to do or say. There is nothing that can take that pain away, but you can certainly provide comfort during the difficult time. Provide a listening ear and maybe a shoulder to cry on. Validate and acknowledge their feelings, keeping in mind that everyone grieves their losses differently.

Check to see if there are any errands that you could cover for a brief time or meals that you could prepare. If they are up for it, get her out of the house and go to lunch or maybe a movie. If your friend or family member has taken pictures of their baby, look at them as you would any other pictures.

Check in with them every now and them and let them know you are thinking about them. Allow them space and quiet time when they request. Also, don't forget the power of silence as sometimes all a person needs is to be in your presence - to have your love, support, and listening ear. Just having a loved one to sit in that uncomfortable space with and not have to worry about discussion. You may not know what to say, and that is okay. Sometimes just being there is enough.

Partners and family – allow yourself your own grief journey as well. For example, if you are a grandparent or were supposed to be a grandparent, you might be hurting for the loss of your grandchild as well as seeing your children in pain from the loss.

<u>Support Groups</u>

Talk is healing and Connection to others can be beneficial to your healing journey. I recommend finding others or a support group in your area as there may be things you have encountered that you never would have otherwise thought like planning a funeral for your baby. It is good to surround yourself with supports who know what you are going through. According death and grief experts Elizabeth Kubler-Ross and David Kessler:

> *"Telling the story helps to dissipate the pain. Telling your story often and in detail is primal to the grieving process. You must get it out. Grief must be witnessed to be healed. Grief shared is grief abated. Support and bereavement groups are important, not only because they allow you to be with others who have experienced loss, but because they provide another forum for talking about the devastating events that befell your world. Tell your tale, because it reinforces that the loss mattered." ~On Grief and Grieving, page 62-63.*

Things won't be the same, but life moves on and you will get through this. I call it, *"Finding your new norm."* Attempting to grieve, to understand why this has happened and trying to learn how to live in the world again, is the start of creating new pathways and possibly making new connections with others whose lives have been turned upside down by losing a baby.

You may never get over it, you will never forget it. The initial shock will eventually fade and intense emotions will begin to subside. But what will never fade is the love. I do not have the answers, but what I do know is that even after days of rain and clouds and dark skies...the sun will shine again. There is hope! There is support!

"How very softly you tiptoed into my world.

Almost silently:

Only for a moment you stayed.

But what an imprint

Your footprints have left

On our Hearts."

~Author Unknown~

Chapter 9: Super Moms

Like a mad competition.

Perfection at is finest. Finest falsehood.

All that you do is never good enough.

I felt that this warranted a chapter: The "Super Mom Syndrome." It is the delusional belief that as moms we are capable of doing everything and all things for all the people in our lives at every single moment of every day while perfectly managing to keep ourselves looking flawless (while most likely inside we are unraveling.) Smile and do it all. Wear your high heels and cook 5 meals and bake treats while holding a baby on each hip and magically packing lunches for the next day, attending five sporting events that evening with perfectly manicured fingers. You go robo-girl…not. Wake up love – you're human.

As for me, ugh, I'm tired writing about these ridiculous standards and expectations we place on ourselves, society places on us, and perhaps what we perceive others expect of us. What about the guilt when women don't feel like they are living up to the standards? It's scary. Some moms don't want to ask for help because they are supposed to be able to do all this.

Another issue of the Super Mom Syndrome: Saying yes, yes, yes, yes, yes, yes, yes, yes, yes, yes, yes, yes, yes, yes…forgetting that "No" is a word in our vocabulary even though we use it daily. "No, don't put your finger in your sister's nose." "No, don't touch the hot stove." "No, honey, the kitty cat doesn't belong in the refrigerator." Oh, so you do know the word! Must learn to appropriately use for yourself also. Trust me, it will save your life.

Especially after growing a child for 9 months and then bringing him/her/them (if multiples) into this world. In our lives, "We have seasons of giving and seasons of receiving…as a new mom, you are in the season of receiving." Birdie Gunyon Meyer, RN, MA Indiana University Health. This is a delicious time in your life for ultimate self-care. You just gave life to a very important, tiny human. You don't have to do it all. There is no need right now to go get your doctorate degree or volunteer at the local food bank or extend yourself to everyone and every place around you.

It is YOUR time to do you, be you, take care of you…so that you can take care of the greatest responsibility in your life right now. You have brought a gift into the world. It took nine months, sometimes longer, of hard work growing a little one inside of you and then to bring the baby into the world in whatever method baby arrived is as exhausting as it is miraculous. It is time to let others help you now. With whatever it might be that you need. Food, chores, someone to hold baby while you shower…

Let us not forget. You are physically healing from pushing a watermelon out of your vagina or having it pulled out of your stomach. You don't bounce back from that overnight.

"It takes a whole village to raise a child but
we need to remember that it was the mother
who had the baby, and she needs our help, too.
~Jane Honikman~

Chapter 10: Myths of Motherhood

- Pregnancy is beautiful and you glow and you will love it.
- You will be a natural mom. It'll come easy.

- You just had a baby, you should be happy.
- Breastfeeding – baby will just crawl up your stomach, find your breast, and have his/her first meal. Then, it'll be easy.
- You will fall in love with your baby instantly. Some women don't right away.
- Babies sleep all the time initially. (What about how they wake up every hour and a half? What about when your engorged breast wake you even if baby is still sleeping? What about when their tummies hurt? What about when they are crying…again?)

- Superwoman Image. You've got to be a perfect wife and mom and housekeeper and if you work – you've got to be awesome at that too and still smile. (Let me know who you are if you exist. I want to interview you.)

- Your breasts are amazingly perky and voluptuous. Okay so maybe. (But ouch, they're technically engorged.)

+ Being a mom is easy breezy. (Insert terrified look emoji).

+ You are Mrs. Fixer Upper. Your job to keep everyone happy and entertain bored children. (Um, no.)

+ Motherhood is the greatest thing in the world and you should love it every single day. (So, motherhood is like life – up, down, clean, messy, crazy, great, dreadful, wonderful…)

+ You should focus all your energy and attention on your children. (If you want to, that's cool. But it is okay to be you and do you. Have hobbies. Work. And it's essential to care for you too first and foremost)

+ Asking for help is a sign of weakness. (It's a sign of strength and bravery)

+ You'll just know. Parenting is pure instinct and will come to you completely naturally. (Hahaha…still laughing…laughing still) … (wait, sorry, on the floor rolling.) It is instinctual as much as learned and trial and error and failed attempts mixed with successes. It's okay if you don't just get it. It's okay if you get it and then one day you don't get it anymore. Parenting is as rewarding as it is difficult and every child and personality will be unique.

Chapter 11: Couples

This goes for all partners of mothers. Male or female. Your relationship is still just as important after birth as it was pre-baby. A common statement after baby: "I miss us."

Plain and simple – after baby, things change.

Intimacy. You won't be having sex for at least 6 weeks after while mom is physically healing. When you do resume intimacy, you might get sprayed by a leaky breast. Maybe you like spontaneity, but sometimes with a baby, you have to schedule and plan around other parenting and household duties. It is so important to keep passion flaming. Realize that it will not be the same as it used to be, but acclimating to rolling over on a toy truck could add humor and is better than your sex life dissolving all together.

Sooo tired. When neither of you are sleeping well, you naturally are not going to be your best selves. You might be more easily frustrated and less tolerating of your partner. Try to alternate night feeding and get rest when you can. Domestic duties increase and can seem overwhelming, but helping one another and not keeping score will be super beneficial. Ask for help, don't just assume. Also, if it's too much, maybe consider hiring a cleaning person for a short time period or check to see you have friends or family who are willing to help.

Raging hormones…enough said.

Figuring out parenting styles. Although this should be a conversation pre-baby, there were probably many things you didn't think about that will arise along the way. Healthy communication and getting on the same page as much as possible will be a huge help.

Your relationship will still need nurturing. Date. Don't forget about date nights. Flirt like you did in the beginning. Tell each other what you appreciate about the other. It brought you together. It brought baby to this world. It will help keep you together. Go out just the two of you. Start a gratitude journal together. Take advantage of tiny moments for a quick kiss. Remind yourselves often of the miracle that was created because of the two of you. Be as kind to yourself and each other through the journey as possible. You both, and your baby, deserve it.

A tidbit from the Gottman Institute. Maintaining a deep friendship with your partner is important. The more familiar you are with your partner, the more intimacy occurs. **Maintain friendship by updating your love maps.**

One of the major discoveries from the BBH research was that if a couple remained good friends during their transition to parenthood, they reported less anger and hostility and felt better equipped to handle the challenges ahead. Keeping up to date with your partner's love maps, or the little details and events of your spouse's life, is critical for connection and intimacy. If you're feeling a bit outdated with one another's love maps, use these **questions** to get re-acquainted. (Eldemire, 2016)

<u>The Love Map Questions from The Gottman Institute</u>

Love Map Exercise:

- Name my two closest friends.

- What was I wearing when we first met?

- Name one of my hobbies.

- What stresses am I facing right now?

- Describe in detail what I did today or yesterday.

- What is my fondest unrealized dream?

- What is one of my greatest fears or disaster scenarios?

- What is my favorite way to spend an evening?

- What is one of my favorite ways to be soothed?

- What is my favorite getaway place?

- What are some of the important events coming up in my life? How do I feel about them?

- What are some of my favorite ways to work out?

- Name one of my major rivals or "enemies."

- What would I consider my ideal job?

- What medical problems do I worry about?

- What was my most embarrassing moment?

- Name one of my favorite novels/movies.

- What is my favorite restaurant?

And an Expansion Pack from Me:

- What is your fondest memory of us?
- What is the first thing I like to do in the morning?
- What is my bedtime routine?
- What is your favorite thing to do with me for fun?
- How do you envision our family's future in the next five years?
- What was my favorite vacation?
- How do I like to relax?
- When is my birthday?
- My favorite season is…
- My favorite flower
- What turns me on?
- Name one of my fondest childhood memories.
- Name someone I admire
- What foods do I hate?
- My favorite animal…
- What song(s) soothes me?
- What song gets me pumped up?
- What restaurant would I want you to take me to for a surprise dinner?
- What snack would you offer me if you notice I'm getting hangry?
- Name something I wouldn't mind binge watching.
- If I were about to donate to an organization, what's my top choice?
- Toilet paper over or under?

<u>Chapter 12: Helping Mom. What Partners, Friends, and Family Can Do</u>

It isn't always easy to watch your loved one when they are struggling and not feeling themselves. You may not always know what to say or do and may feel helpless. Here are some tips when you're feeling lost.

- Believe her.
- Don't just talk to baby when you visit. Address mom too.
- Reassure her.
    - "This is not your fault."
    - "You are not alone."
    - "You'll get better."
- Encourage her to talk about her feelings.
- Let her know she is heard.
- Educate yourself on postpartum mental health.
- Help with housework before she asks. Some moms don't like to ask or feel like they are being a burden or just don't have the motivation or energy to ask. Don't expect accolades. If you're helping, it's because you want to help.
- Withhold any judgement or criticism.
- Encourage her to take time for herself.
- If she is home all day, don't expect her to have everything spotless. It's okay if all she gets done is one thing today. Raising a baby is work

and raising a baby when you're not feeling yourself is even harder.

- Help her reach out for supports if needed.
- Offer resources without being too pushy.
- Ask. Don't avoid.
    - "Could you use a hug?"
    - "How can I help?"
- And sometimes Do. Just do her laundry. If you know she likes the body pillow in bed, put it there for her right before she crawls in exhausted. Make her favorite tea or coffee for when she wakes up.
- Make sure she is taking care of herself too and not just baby and everyone else. If you notice she hasn't had anything to eat all day, prepare something for her or order. Keeps healthy snacks handy for her. Low sugar = low mood and irritability. Especially if breastfeeding – it's important she nourish herself too.
- Open and honest communication.
- Allow and respect time alone if she wants it or needs a little space.
- Offer to go to doctor appointments with her.
- Set boundaries for yourself. If she is too upset, ask to return to the conversation later when you're both calmer.
- Let her pamper herself without feeling bad about it. Let's shift our negative conversations from: "Why is she getting her toes done? She

should be home resting." "I can't believe you want to go to the store when we have chores to do here." Or whatever...to… "You work so hard. You're a great mom. You deserve to pamper yourself." "I'm so proud of you." "You don't get enough time for you. How about a massage or hot bath?" Catching my drift? Moms spend so much time loving and nurturing the world. Let's reciprocate the love they radiate.

- Celebrate her successes.
- Bring her meals.
- Keep in contact.
- Keep inviting her to things even if she can't go this time, maybe next.
- It's okay to take it day by day, moment by moment.
- If you're starting a statement with "At least…" then it's probably not something you should be saying. Just saying.
- Know that every woman's timeline in recovery is different. Don't compare her to others and allow her to have her own sacred journey without rushing her or saying things like, "Shouldn't you feel better now."
- Take care of you too! It's not easy to see your loved one hurting or struggling. You are a precious gift too and to be there for her as well, it is wise for you to prioritize your own self-

care too. Example, if you just spent all day helping her with chores and baby and it's time to go home…give her a hug (if she wants), say your "see you laters," and then when you get home, be sure you eat, relax, skip your to-do list until tomorrow if necessary, and get a good night sleep.

For family members wanting to better understand and have more resources and guidance on how to support loved ones, I would like to recommend Jane Honikman's book: *"I'm Listening. A Guide to Supporting Postpartum Families."*

Chapter 13: Treatment Modalities

I am going to get all technical for a brief moment and then in the next section of this book, I will give you some of my own tid-bits of helpful information you can use at home.

First, let me start off with an observation. I have unfortunately seen and encountered gaps in care. Pregnant women and/or breast feeding women go to their OB. Their OB sends them to a psychiatrist, but because they are pregnant or breast feeding, the psychiatrist sends them back to their OB. They fall through the gap and often don't always get the help they need. Some call for help and are told there is a 3 month waiting list or worse, longer, or they don't have openings for new patients, or they don't treat perinatal mood disorders. I hope this doesn't happen to you. If you find yourself having a difficult time, search online for professionals who specialize in this area and/or check out Postpartum Support International at www.postpartum.net. Don't give up. Finding good help will be a wonderful asset in your healing. If you are struggling and it is too exhausting and overwhelming to deal with all that, ask a friend or family member to help you find someone. Sometimes people find a great fit quickly. I just don't want to see you lose hope if this doesn't happen right away.

There are many options in care from individual therapy which might be one hour per week to intensive outpatient which can range from a few hours a few days a week. Women with postpartum psychosis will need more intensive, inpatient, overnight care until they are back on their feet. Below are some of the types of therapy that vary based on what you want/need and what the therapist provides.

A few of the more common types of therapy:

CBT – Cognitive Behavioral Therapy

Emphasizes the link between thoughts and feelings as well as identifying negative/challenging thought patterns (cognitive distortions) and building healthier thought processes. Recognizing how our thoughts affect our feelings and behaviors and how to improve our thinking to therefore improve how we feel.

DBT – Dialectical Behavior Therapy

Learning new skills to help regulate emotions, decreasing conflict, and dealing with intense/painful emotions. Mindfulness, acceptance, and distress tolerance are some key aspects of DBT.

EMDR – Eye Movement Desensitization and Reprocessing.

A specialized treatment by trained professionals in which one is asked to recall distressing images while generating one type of bilateral sensory input, typically side-to-side eye movements. This is especially beneficial for those with previous trauma or birth related trauma.

Interpersonal Therapy – works on understanding how your mood impacts your relationships. Focuses on effective communication and problem solving.

<u>Transcranial Magnetic Stimulation (TMS)</u> – uses magnetic not electrical currents. Intensive. Daily for 8 weeks.

<u>Freespira</u> – for anxiety/panic. I recently began working with this company at my private practice. It is an FDA-cleared, medication free treatment option covered by some insurances. It is a breathing system that patients take home for 4 weeks in a small bag (reminds me of a lunch bag) with an electronic tablet that provides instructions. 15 minutes, twice a day. It helps stabilize breathing patterns, increase exhaled carbon dioxide and decrease panic attacks.

<u>Group Therapy</u> – meetings with other women experiencing similar issues that together you can talk, sympathize, relate, and help one another grow, learn, and heal.

<u>Family Therapy</u> – family members are involved in sessions. Can be helpful so that others are educated on postpartum mental illness. A woman can work on her relationships with other members especially if there are some sources of stress. Communication Skills. Tips for family on how they can provide the best support.

<u>Couple's Therapy</u> – if you have tension in your relationship, this can be a great option or even if your partner wants to learn more about what you are going through or you would like them to be educated. Communication skills. Improve your relationship. Adapting to lifestyle changes that occur after baby. How to be a couple now that two have become more.

Psychiatry

As far as Medication Management…For this you will need to see a Psychiatrist. Not all women will need medication. There really is no "go-to" medication and no "one size fits all." The best one to take will be the one that works. You and your doctor will figure this out together. The goal is to eliminate risk and control symptoms. Every person's chemistry and make-up is different and depending on whether you are experiencing more depression verses anxiety or vice versa or equally both, or bipolar symptoms and need a mood stabilizer as well, or psychosis in which hospitalization is necessary and antipsychotics. That's why it will be essential that you keep in contact with your doctor and keep the communication open and honest. That way they can help you find what works for you.

If you are pregnant or breastfeeding, is does not mean that meds are not an option for you. They can be incredibly beneficial and it all comes down to risk verses benefits. AJOG, the American Journal of Obstetrics and Gynecology states that "When a psychiatric condition necessitates pharmacotherapy, the benefits of such therapy far outweigh the potential minimal risks."

Alternative Treatment Options

Some women seek other treatments such as listed below. Everyone is unique. Please consult with your physician and decide what is best for you.

These may not all be supported by research as proven treatments, however, they have been reported by some women, myself included to work or help alleviate symptoms.

I started taking a little orange chewy square, Omega-3 Vitamin, from a nutrition store. Some supplements are not healthy during breastfeeding. Always consult with a physician before taking anything.

- Float Tank - pregnancy and after
- Essential Oils
- Yoga
- Acupuncture
- Hypnotherapy
- Seek guidance of a professional if considering herbal remedies.

On The Horizon

Fancy a Blueberry Cocktail?

At Canada's leading brain science institute, the Campbell Family Mental Health Research Institute (CAMH), Dr. Jeffrey Meyer, head of the neuroimaging program in mood and anxiety, has been researching a cocktail of nutrients. A blueberry cocktail that is and it consists of blueberry extract, blueberry juice and the amino acids tryptophan and tyrosine. The hope is that this supplementation kit will ward off baby blues by correcting a chemical imbalance that naturally happens in the brain a few days after birth. In his recent study, women did not experience depressive symptoms after birth when they took four doses. (Bilodeau, 2017).

> Meyer says the supplements work because they are building blocks for brain chemicals that are naturally depleted after birth. He explains that there's a protein in the brain called monoamine oxidase A, or MAO-A, that renders useless three chemicals that usually help to manage our moods: serotonin, norepinephrine and dopamine.
>
> (Bilodeau, 2017).

There is still research in the works with a follow up double-blind study. I am curious and anxious to hear more about this as updates become available. Please do not just go out and buy supplements to try on your own. Do you remember what happened in Willy Wonka? But seriously though, even with supplements, the right dose and timing is critical. Please seek medical advisement.

<u>Hummingbird Study</u>

At the 2017 PSI (Postpartum Support International Conference) in Philadelphia, PA, I was first enlightened about the Hummingbird Study and told was a study worth watching unfold. When wrapping up this book in 2018, I saw a Facebook post by a friend that gave me hope that this had finally become a reality. She was sweetly praising her husband who serves as Chair of the FDA Psychopharmacologic Drugs Advisory Committee for encouraging not just this new treatment, but its use on mother baby units as opposed to stand alone adult inpatient centers. I opened the article after reading her post. I was so excited to see this all come to fruition. I know, I know. You're waiting to hear what on earth it is and why I'm ecstatic. So what is all this hype?

It is a breakthrough IV medication, Brexanolone - 60-hour infusion for the treatment of postpartum depression. A formulation of allopregnanolone, a neurosteroid described as "appositive allosteric modulator of gamma-aminobutryic acid A (GABA) receptors." (Tucker, 2018).

If successful, it would be the first antidepressant approved specifically for PPD. Flash forward from that conference I attended, the preliminary results were presented at the American Psychiatric Association in May 2018. From what I have read about the studies and results, I am probably most excited about the speed of the results. My heart always has a twinge of pain in it when I tell women, who just want to enjoy their baby but are hurting so much, that their antidepressant is going to take 2-4 weeks to really kick in to notice results. They've been struggling long enough already. Even one day with postpartum is one day too many. Brexanolone begins to work within a few days. It does have to be administered intravenously by qualified specialists and therefore will need to be in a hospital verses taking an oral antidepressant at home.

<u>Just a few quotes from the pros to wrap this up:</u>

"I think it could be of tremendous help in changing the trajectory for postpartum depression," said panel chair Rajesh Narendran, MD, attending psychiatrist at the Resolve Crisis Network and associate professor in radiology and psychiatry at the University of Pittsburgh, Pennsylvania. (Tucker, 2018).

The results "confirm and extend the previous work showing that brexanolone has a rapid onset of action that is unlike anything else currently available," said Dr. Samantha Meltzer-Brody from the University of North Carolina at Chapel Hill School of Medicine. (Boggs, 2018).

Dr. Michael E. Silverman from Icahn School of Medicine at Mount Sinai, in New York City: "Brexanolone as a treatment for PPD is a potentially exciting avenue; indeed, as clinicians we could use more options in our treatment toolbox," Dr. Silverman said. "I'm hopeful additional work, including replications of the above study to clarify the reported findings, will continue to be conducted." (Lancet 2018).

<u>Chapter 14: Mother Baby Units</u>

In my heart there was an ache when women would tell me they went to a general facility for treatment, but it made it worse. Some were treated poorly and many reported not getting proper treatment as staff were not trained specifically in postpartum and they were thrown into a mix of everything from substance abuse, schizophrenia, and suicidal behaviors.

I was thrilled to hear at the Postpartum Support International - PSI Conference, about the facility in North Carolina offering just that – specialty care for perinatal mental health. The United States' first, free-standing perinatal psychiatric unit at University of North Carolina hospital in Chapel Hill. The inpatient program is specifically for postpartum women. A place that "gets" women after birth. An understanding of specific needs as well as the importance of incorporating mother-infant bonding and attachment and not just ripping her away from her baby completely while she is in the hospital.

I had always wondered why moms were removed from their infants if they needed inpatient treatment. What if they were breastfeeding? What about bonding?

In the UK there are several Mother-and-Baby units. They are on the rise in Ireland. The first Mother-Baby Unit (MBU) in France opened in 1979 and in Belgium in 1990. (Cazas & Glangeaud-Freudenthal, 2010).

In July 2009, the first MBU in India was started at the National Institute of Mental Health and Neurosciences (NIMHANS). A five bedded facility for admitting mother-infant dyads with a multidisciplinary team of psychiatrists, psychiatric social workers, nurses, lactation experts, and pediatric support is available from a neighboring pediatric hospital. (Chandra et al., 2015).

Many places have beneficial facilities to help our wonderful mommas and I hope that other countries will be open to opening centers like this as well, including my home country. If you are struggling after having your baby, check to see if there is a Mother-Baby Unit near you or even a place offering specialized care with trained professionals in postpartum mood and anxiety disorders.

One last place I will discuss that has excellent center for postpartum depression is right here next to me in Pittsburgh, PA. Freshly opened in 2018, Allegheny Health Network and the Alexis Joy D'Achille Foundation, collaborated to open the Alexis Joy D'Achille Center for Perinatal Mental Health at West Penn Hospital. This new facility provides care to women with pregnancy-related mental health while allowing them to be with their infant. (Torrance, 2018). Below is my experience touring this wonderful facility.

<u>January 24, 2019 – Tour of West Penn Hospital's Perinatal Mental Health Center</u>

I woke up to some beautiful, heavy wet snowflakes in the morning. A nice serene view for the drive. Perfect weather to reflect in during my walk from my parked car to the hospital.

Today I visited West Penn Hospital to see the new Perinatal Mental Health Center. The grand opening was held recently on December 18, 2018 and has been in the works the last year, made possible by the collaboration between Allegheny Health Network (AHN) and the Alexis Joy D'Achille Foundation.

I was greeted by two friendly staff members, one of whom gave me a tour and talked about the center. It provides individual therapy as well as intensive outpatient care and is set up so that women with perinatal depression and other anxiety and mood disorders can bring their baby while receiving treatment. There are activities such as infant yoga, infant massage, and infant bonding for moms to do with baby in addition to therapy. It caters to not just women, but to helping partners and other family members. They also have received additional services to offer childcare. One less worry and stressor for moms as the center is helping to alleviate boundaries that may impede upon women receiving treatment.

The most moving part of my tour was when I stepped into the waiting room and looked at the large, black and white photo of Alexis Joy D'Achille. A lovely woman who unfortunately lost her battle to postpartum depression nearly six weeks after delivering her first child. Her husband Steven began to spread awareness of postpartum mental health and created the Alexis Joy D'Achille Foundation, which also hosts fundraisers and has helped create the center I visited today. Her spirit lives on and is a light to other women and families. My heart aches for the struggle she must have had and the pain of postpartum depression. It is real and it can be a horrifying occurrence that mommas don't deserve to experience, but some of us unfortunately are blindsided by it. Systemically, it also impacts the woman's family and the center is here to help them as well.

I have been wanting to attend the *"Night of Joy"* black tie gala hosted by the Alexis Joy D'Achille Foundation and this year I am making it a priority to be there. It is a fundraiser that is held the weekend of Alexis' birthday in April to celebrate her life and continue a legacy, raising awareness and helping other women and families.

For more information, please visit the following sites:

https://www.ahn.org/specialties/womens-health/womens-behavioral-health

http://www.alexisjoyfoundation.org/

https://www.wpxi.com/news/top-stories/allegheny-health-network-opens-area-s-first-postpartum-depression-prenatal-mental-health-center/890715145

Chapter 15: Our Dynamic Duo: Life on the other side of PeriWrinkle

We are a balance of dirt and high heels.
Nature and Fancy events.
Swimming in a creek to snorkeling in the Caribbean.
Being busy to spending a day at home doing nothing.
We travel the world and sprinkle love wherever we go.
We laugh. We cry. We persevere. We do it all together.
Our Dynamic Duo.
My sweet Skyla and I.

It sucks being in the midst of PeriWrinkle and feeling like there is no hope. When people tell you, like I am now, about life on the other side, but you can't see it … I know… I was there. In utter disbelief. But it still needs said because somewhere in me it resonated. That tiny voice saying, "You'll be okay." The encouraging thought, "you'll get better." I needed to know, when I didn't feel it and couldn't see it, that it was there. That, when I was ready, I could start putting it in the front of my focus, choosing it, being it, and living the hope. It doesn't matter your speed. Moving forward at whatever pace is in your unique journey. Movement, not speed, is vital! Even if you hop not leap, or do a shuffle instead of a step...I am so proud of you! It is a big deal and it's again, movement. Moving toward your future.

I can't even imagine and never want to think about how my daughter's world would not have been the same and all I would have missed out on if I let postpartum continue to be in the driver's seat. There came a point when

I had enough and it was time for PeriWrinkle to move the heck over and out the window.

God gifted me a beautiful little soul and I live everyday now to raise her the best I can. She and I fill our home with love and positivity and welcome nothing less.

I love seeing the new things she takes interest in that I never did. As much as I help teach her and help her learn, she most certainly enlightens my universe every day. Dragons. Archery. The neat things she learns at school and can't wait to share with me about all the different types of clouds, that bears don't actually hibernate they just go into torpor (deep sleep), and so on. Friends of mine were never really into car racing until their son came along and developed his own interest. Now, they go to races together as a family. So, as parents we broaden our horizon. How lucky we are that our children help us grow!

Seeing things again as though for the first time can happen through the eyes of a child if you allow yourself to be open and immerse yourself in their world, just as much as they acclimate to yours. There is so much good on the other side of PeriWrinkle.

I have traveled to places I never imagined I would go. Chasing Dragons on the Emerald Island of Ireland. We've been to the Dominican Republic twice. I was headed to Niagara Falls and thanks to my darling Skyla, we also ended up at the *Poop Café* in Canada. (Once again I was very, VERY enlightened). Next she wants to go to Greece and I want to go to Italy. She's bummed I went to Iceland without her, so I promised I would take her soon. Yellowstone. London ... The world is yet to be graced by me and my sweet gal. Postpartum didn't have a chance at ruining a great life for the two of us!!!

Not everyone will want a life like this. This is what I have chosen and what works with my daughter as well. Some people are more home bodies. Some people will want to ski in the Alps (not me, burr). Maybe read a gazillion books together. Do artwork together. Although my child is a talented young artist, I am not. This will not be something we ever excel at together, haha and that's okay, but she will and I love watching her. When you are struggling right now and anxiety makes you wonder if you are a good mom or if you are doing everything right…try to push away those thoughts just for a moment and instead imagine what you and your child might be doing together someday. Imagine what interests they might develop. Write it down and maybe do a time capsule and open it up ten years later.

If you are having trouble bonding and forming an attachment with your baby because of PeriWrinkle, I encourage you to keep trying and want to let you know that there is no better time than now. It is not too late. Seek help and live the life you and your child were born to live together. Your future together is waiting. Savor the precious now and get excited about what is next.

"You're off to Great Places!
Today is your day!
Your mountain is waiting,
So... get on your way!"
Dr. Seuss: Oh, The Places You'll Go!

Chapter 16: A Quick Word for the Pros

As professionals, I think we should ask and keep asking. Don't take her first "I'm fine. Everything is great!" as a sign that she is doing well. Underneath the smile, might be a storm. Meet her where she is and walk beside her from there. No matter what profession you are. Screen for everything, not just postpartum depression. Ask and ask again. Ask the important questions. Ask the tough questions. Whether you are:

OB's	Pediatricians	Midwives
Doulas	Childbirth Educators	Counselors
Psychologists	Psychiatrists	Lactation Consultants
	And more	

Many times in my childbirth classes, when I would discuss this topic, people would get quiet and/or look away. Not many people want to acknowledge it. As if avoidance will create an immunity to it. I hope professionals are seeing past the denial. Our mommas and their babies deserve our best care.

And likewise, so do you! You deserve to know that you are amazing for what you do, all the help you provide, and the hard work. Maybe you don't see it or feel it every day, but you are a gift and in the place you are at for a reason. Keep doing what you do. I am proud of you! You are needed and much appreciated.

Chapter 17: Royal family

This chapter is a quick shout out to the British Royal Family. I just adore them and their openness with talking about issues such as perinatal mood disorders.

I perhaps might be a bit partial too because my DNA results revealed that Great Britain was my number one highest match and it sure has helped me in this journey to connect me to my roots and keep them refined.

Maternal Mental Health. Talking about it, normalizing it, and making it known to the world will hopefully decrease anxiety and feeling alone for women who struggle with these issues as well as hopefully allow society to let go of the negativity and decrease the stigma. We need to talk about these things.

In November of 2017 Kate Middleton, this is what the Duchess of Cambridge did. She hosted a private round table meeting at Kensington Palace to address maternal mental health. Because Mums matter! Because open discussions about it are fruitful.

A Tweet from **Kensington Palace** (@KensingtonRoyal)

> If left untreated, maternal mental health problems can have significant and long lasting effect on the woman and her family.
> At least 20% of women are affected by mental health problems during pregnancy or in the first year following the birth of a child.

Even being a princess or a queen won't grow you an immunity against postpartum. Princess status won't even build you a proverbial wall of protection lined with the strongest soldiers that fight off all attacks of unwanted intrusive thoughts, mood changes, and worries. Sometimes, it happens. No one in this world possesses a force field against it. It doesn't discriminate. Not even ME, a therapist, was protected against it. I was blindsided. But no matter whether you experience it or not or to whatever degree, there is help and there is most certainly hope. It is not your fault. You didn't choose this. So, princess or not, put on your crown sweetheart. You are an amazing and phenomenal woman. Time to fight postpartum with your pink high heels and fairy dust - AKA – your support system and awesome treatment team.

To the royals who are also helping get out the word about maternal mental health. It exists; it's real. Mums matter. Babies matter. Partners and the families matter. Love my tea – I'll have a cuppa and drink to that!

<u>Elle Magazine 11-2-17</u>:

> The Duchess - who was the brainchild of mental health campaign Heads Together with her husband Prince William and brother-in-law Prince Harry - has spoken openly about her own struggles with the isolation of motherhood following the birth of her children, Prince George and Princess Charlotte.

Speaking with mothers during a meeting at the Global Academy earlier this year, the pregnant mum admitted to a group of mothers: 'It is lonely at times and you do feel quite isolated, but actually so many other mothers are going through exactly what you are going through.

Go Prince Williams and Princess Kate! Not that I didn't love you enough before, but you've won me over even more.

May we all spread the word with a loving demeanor and offer support. May we not ostracize our mommas or leave them feeling all alone in the dark.

Chapter 18: Mother Wolf

My love of wolves began in college when my professor and life role model, Terry Kasecamp, introduced me to the book: "*Women Who Run with the Wolves: Myths and Stories of the Wild Woman Archetype*," by Clarissa Pinkola Estés. I am forever grateful to her as this book continues to pop up in my life in beneficial ways.

This love carried on when I went to a zoo that just happened to have, not just wolves, but baby wolves and I got to hold them. I still have that photo and treasure it. I grew fond of these beautiful creatures.

My wolf love affair continued and in November 2016 I visited the *Wolf Sanctuary of PA* and stayed on sight at the bed and breakfast, Speedwell Forge, in Lititz, Pennsylvania...right in the center of the refuge for wolves. To hear them howl at night from your bedroom…Calling to one another. It was a surreal, breathtaking, and beautiful experience.

Then, I held an empowering women's workshop based on Estés' book early in 2017. So, when deciding on a cover for this book, it was hardly a thought. It came natural. I closed my eyes and the first thing I envisioned was me and my daughter standing with a pack of wolves or even one wolf. Strong, loving, intuitive women! As my daughter corrects everyone, wolves do not howl at the moon. They howl to communicate with one another. A web of interconnected social stability. Why do wolves howl? "Love scientists say…a serious case of puppy love," (Dye, 2013).

How essential for those of us going through PeriWrinkle and needing our support networks. Finding our howl, connecting with others who can help us and who have been through it, learning to ask for help, and continuing to persevere. I interviewed a woman for the "stories" section of this book and she discussed the "Wolf Hour." Then I interviewed a dad who acquired the nickname the "Wolf" in college. All these things sealed the deal for me. I knew a wolf needed to be on the cover.

Thanks to *Ironwood Wolves* in Ohio and photographer, Rachel Lauren … that vision came true, mostly. Because of safety, my daughter was not in the shoot, but watched from a distance and said one day when she is old enough, she too wants a wolf encounter too. I am so grateful for the surreal and amazing experience. When Rachel sent me the final edits, I fell in love with the photo of the wolf howling as well as the big wolf kisses that looked like he was smoothing out my wrinkles – Periwrinkles. Tough decision.

In honor of all this, I thought it was only necessary to have a small segment on wolves. Some people give them a bad rap. They are actually quite amazing. First, I will take you behind the scenes of the photoshoot for the front cover and then I will talk about mother wolves and their similarities to humans.

Behind the Scenes with Logan the Wolf

It was Valentine's Day, February 14, 2019. I put my daughter on the bus and I needed some beautification. The lovely Nicole Angotti did my hair and later I picked up Skyla from school and we drove to Columbus, Ohio. It was like waiting for Christmas Day. The day couldn't come soon enough and the drive wasn't short enough. We arrived finally though and met with Ironwood Wolves. Rachel Lauren was my photographer and her partner helped with Logan - the handsome, debonair wolf. My furry Valentine. What a beauty. He remained on a leash the entire time. (Edited out of the photo). Can't have a wild animal on the loose. I was not expecting that I would be able to get too close or touch him, but Logan broke the ice with an amazing introduction – a big, wet kiss. I laughed. It was marvelous. I never wanted to wash my face again. Just kidding. But really, I loved his sweet, affectionate kisses and that he kept sneaking them in throughout the entire shoot. I got to touch him and pet him and pose with him. His fur was thick and glorious and those paws!!! So big it keeps you humbled. He was very curious as the owners described. Alert to different movements and sounds. The absolute coolest, unexpected part was when a siren went off and he began to howl. Right beside me. The sound. The energy that flooded my body. The intense, raw, genuine nature in front of me. It was magical and unlike anything I have ever experienced. I am so grateful for the opportunity. I am appreciative that Logan accepted and embraced me. What wonderful creatures. No, I am not saying go approach a wolf in the wild or have one as a pet. They tend to be more wary of humans, but remember, they are still wild animals. This experienced happened to be with trained professionals and a trained animal.

Momma Wolves:

Female wolves prepare for motherhood in similar ways to humans. During pregnancy that work on their relationship with their mate and enjoy last moments of cuddle time, playing and hunting together before their time and attention will soon be shared with babies. She prepares for birth, searching for and creating the perfect den, a process similar to nesting in humans.

When it is time, motherly instincts take over and the wolf will give birth, chew off the umbilical cord, and lick her sweet baby pups clean. She also eats the placenta and replenishes nourishment for herself in preparation to nurse her pups.

The very protective momma will continue caring for her babes and not letting them out of the den for at least three to four weeks. During that time, she remains with them as self-care, healing and recovery is important as well. (Katya, 2015).

Also, a guarantee that if this protective momma is met with a threat, her nose will be Peri -Wrinkled – a clear statement for predators to back off. To all you loving and protective mommas, you are amazing, you are beautiful, you are stronger than you know. Like the wolf – be nurturing, be gentle, be playful, be curious, be adaptable, be you. And don't forget to rely on your pack. We can't do it all alone. Be friendly and loving to each other and care for each other and yourself. When you don't feel strong, stand up tall (literally, get up, stand up). I want you to put your chin up toward the sky, stretch your arms out far (power pose) and (no, you don't have to howl), but imagine yourself as a playful, confident wolf. Breathe in goodness and intuition and breathe out stress, fears, and pressures. And as you exhale, stretch yourself out a little more and reach your chin up higher.

A few final words from the lovely Clarissa Pinkola Estés:

> "Healthy wolves and healthy women share certain psychic characteristics: keen sensing, playful spirit, and a heightened capacity for devotion. Wolves and women are relational by nature, inquiring, possessed of great endurance and strength. They are deeply intuitive, intensely concerned with their young, their mates, and their pack. They are experienced in adapting to constantly changing circumstances; they are fiercely stalwart and very brave."

General Wolf Rules For Life
1. Eat
2. Rest
3. Rove in between
4. Render loyalty
5. Love the children
6. Cavil in the moonlight
7. Tune your ears
8. Attend to the bones
9. Make love
10. Howl

Part II – Our Stories

Thank You

This next segment of the book is dedicated to real people who have encountered PeriWrinkle in some way or another. I decided not to interview anyone who may have been a client of mine in therapy at this time, although there are so many delightful women who I knew would have helped contribute. I ventured outside of work.

I want to say thank you to the wonderful contributors. I am honored that you have allowed me to listen to your story and to share it here. Sharing your story, our stories, it isn't always easy. It can make you feel raw and vulnerable. It can bring back memories that might be difficult or even painful.

It can also help and heal. I am so grateful to all of the people I have met along my journey and to the ones who are a part of this book.

In your journey, in your healing, you are not alone.

<u>Cindy – 2-7-17 – Southwestern Pennsylvania</u>

"A diagnosis would have helped. I knew something was desperately wrong."

Cindy is a good spirited woman that lights up the room. She is always considerate of others and presents with a smile. She is the woman I spoke of earlier that I saw and overheard across a room one time at an event. It made me feel so much better about what I was going through and that I wasn't alone. She was first on my list to interview when I decided to write this book.

Cindy delivered her first child in 1991. After baby's arrival, she said she wasn't happy and didn't want to be alone. It was an awful feeling. She couldn't eat or sleep. She would wake up hot. Not sleep for two days, then sleep good. Her language slowed. Her hands were curled – so tense. Anxiety was high too.

She had also had a cesarean section and the back of her legs would burn and sweat. It was an unexpected and unplanned surgery as they discovered that the cord was wrapped around her baby's neck. I asked if this trauma may have contributed to her postpartum depression and she said maybe, but it was hard to tell.

She had a wonderful life, but she just didn't feel herself. She ended up going to a local hospital for a few minute interview and the doctor scared her. "He just didn't have a clue" as he told her that she would end up in their mental ward and "You don't want to go there, do you?"

How awful to need help, but not be able to get it and to then encounter professionals who you think you can trust, who just don't get it and do not provide the help you desperately need.

Two weeks passed and she was not feeling better so she went to a larger hospital facility in the nearest city and spent one month on the inpatient unit where they said she had "textbook classic postpartum depression." Back then, she was given Nortriptyline, a tricyclic antidepressant and Elavil. She went home and her heart was pounding so hard. The male doctor did his best she said, but then she was blessed with a female doctor from England who immediately recognized that the medications she was put on was causing the issue and she was then prescribed blood pressure medication. The doctor from England was understanding and compassionate and she specialized in treating women and knew the combination of meds that worked. This was huge in Cindy's treatment and care.

There was such a stigma and she remembers it also being hard because "they take your baby away." When you are in the hospital awhile, it is hard. One night without baby is hard and almost impossible for women to breastfeed if they can have their baby. She learned from her female doctor that they were more advanced in England and had special units just for mothers and babies so they didn't have to be apart. Here, she said, you were just thrown into a mix of everything and without your baby.

Cindy went on to have another beautiful baby and no perinatal mood issues as she and her medical team were proactive starting medication almost immediately after birth. She took her meds only for four weeks and was feeling fine so she stopped and was okay after that. Her children are now amazing adults. She was warned that menopause might be problematic with a history of menopause, but for her, she was blessed with no symptoms during menopause. Cindy is an example that there is hope on the other side of PeriWrinkle.

<u>Things that <u>helped</u> and Tips from Cindy</u>

- "Medication and CBT (Cognitive Behavioral Therapy) go hand in hand."
- Early recognition
- Seek the highest medical treatment available with specialists in women's mental health.
- Read up on it and if you cannot concentrate because of the depression, have someone help you research and learn about the symptoms and what to do.
- Support Network after hospital: "My family really helped."
- "Don't Blame Yourself." It is a real condition.
- Search for help high and low and don't be afraid to go get help.

<u>Haley - March 4, 2017</u>

Today I met Hayley at Starbucks at the Waterfront just south of Pittsburgh.

She is a lovely, sweet lady with beautiful brown hair, sparkling eyes and a radiant smile. If I had just met her randomly today at a coffee shop, I never would have guessed that she had struggled with postpartum depression, which is a strong testament to the hope on the other side of postpartum depression.

I learned today that her story had went public as she discussed being on television for WPXI news and in the local paper. I was happy to hear this. Not happy that she had to go through what she did, but that her story was given a broader audience, that her voice was heard, and I hope this book allows her story to reach and help many others.

Haley kept the gender a surprise and was excited for delivery day to discover what she was having. She gave birth to a son, Brayden, who is now nineteen months old (at time of interview). He was welcomed into the world to Hayley and her husband Tim's loving arms on August 12, 2015, a few weeks ahead of schedule. At first things were okay, but two weeks after bringing her baby boy home, Hayley noticed some changes. It was also around the time that people disappeared, so to speak. The visits from family were less frequent and her husband went back to work. She found herself sad and crying and stated: "I felt I couldn't soothe baby." Things felt like they were going downhill.

As a new mom, she was hard on herself. It is tough to live up to cultural standards of "Super Mom" and feeling like you should know it all and be able to do it all, all on your own. She felt like she had to be strong and didn't want to ask for help. Yet, the reality is, as Hayley reported, it really does take a village to raise a child.

Haley decided to seek treatment before things got worse and said that therapy and medication made a huge impact. Her husband was very supportive.

To women out there struggling with PMAD, Haley wants you to know that there is so much hope and it is not your fault. "Postpartum depression is a very real thing." She is grateful for those who took her seriously and for clinicians who provided excellent treatment.

Beth

Beth is one cool cat, that's for sure. She is one of the kindest women I know which breaks my heart, some of what she went through. However, it has been amazing to witness triumph through her journey and to see her shine as a classy and down-to-earth momma of two now. Here is her story (written in 2017):

My postpartum depression started before I was pregnant, but I didn't realize this until months later. I was also in denial of my depression until I was 7 months postpartum, telling myself that my symptoms were due to extreme exhaustion and an extremely high needs baby.

I had a miscarriage in February 2015, a little over a year before my daughter's birth. I never fully grieved my loss, which was traumatic. I had symptoms throughout my pregnancy which were dismissed at each prenatal appointment, and I in turn minimized and denied what I was feeling because I trusted the midwives and doctors I was seeing. A week before we found out about the miscarriage, I was in a minor car accident and went to the local ER for reassurance. The nurse and doctor missed the miscarriage – the nurse told me he found the baby's heartbeat after some difficulty. Although I wasn't convinced, I was full of relief and decided to trust what he said. I called my OB the next day to see if I should come in for a check and was told not to since I had been discharged from the ER.

We found out on February 10 at our scheduled 18 week anatomy scan there was no heartbeat. We already knew our baby was a girl, and she had a name. The doctor said it appeared she stopped growing 3 weeks prior. I can still feel all of those raw emotions now – the way my hope and excitement was immediately replaced with shock, disbelief, and confusion. It's still hard for me to comprehend how things can change so suddenly, how so much can be taken away in a split second. I look back on that day and wonder why I didn't realize there was no heartbeat as soon as the nurse started the ultrasound, why I didn't instinctually know something was wrong when she asked me if I had been feeling alright and notice any symptoms, when she excused herself to get the doctor. I'm so thankful my husband was with me that day because I don't know what I would have done without him.

We discussed my options with the doctor and I was scheduled for a D/C the following morning. A few hours before we needed to be at the hospital I miscarried at home. I was in pain, scared, and overwhelmed with grief. I can still feel the horrible pain, and frequently relive that awful moment.

The next few months were difficult; I was overcome with bouts of intense anger, easily triggered when I saw pregnant women or babies, and struggling to hold everything together. On the outside I acted like things were fine, that I was ok and moving forward. My husband knew better – I know he probably walked on eggshells much of the time and never knew when to anticipate my next mood swing.

We talked about getting pregnant again and started trying as soon as we could. I found out on Father's Day I was pregnant and was immediately filled with joy and excitement. But I was also terrified and spent the first trimester anticipating the worst. I didn't eat well and stopped exercising - I had done this religiously during my first pregnancy and told myself it made no difference. I had such horrible morning sickness that I spent almost the entire first trimester inside the house on the couch because the heat and humidity instantly triggered intense exhaustion and nausea. I also had my husband come to every prenatal appointment during the first trimester, and until I could feel our daughter move, because I was terrified of being alone in case anything went wrong. I also had no idea I was depressed, because I was happy - being pregnant was everything I wanted.

I received all prenatal care at a free-standing birth center because I lost trust in traditional Western medicine and interventions. I was terrified of being in a hospital delivery room and didn't want any doctors present for the birth. I planned to deliver with no medical interventions and no medication. At 40 weeks when I hadn't delivered yet I was automatically scheduled for medical induction. I tried every natural and homeopathic means of induction possible, including acupuncture, prenatal massage, eating TONS of pineapple, evening primrose oil, and really weird and awkward pregnant sex. I delivered on March 2 at 41+1 weeks, a beautiful and intense natural birth. Since we delivered at the birth center, we were home the same day. I had tested positive for Group B strep and we were given instructions to monitor our daughter at home that night and the following day. During my 24 hour follow-up phone call, I told the midwife everything was great and I was happy, because I was. During our 48 hour in-home visit we learned our daughter was jaundice, but reassured not to worry and instructed to practice lots of skin to skin contact and time by the sun. We ended up admitting her to the pediatric intensive care unit the same day and spent 2 very long nights there.

Looking back now I think that experience really triggered my depression. Despite everything, we ended up in a hospital and I was terrified something horrible would happen. Her bilirubin levels were so high the doctors had discussed blood transfusions if she didn't respond to the light therapy quickly. I sat and watched helplessly as 2 nurses struggled more than 4 times to insert her IV, all while she was screaming and crying. I laid in bed at night feeling helpless when I couldn't pick her up and hold her or nurse her while she cried and screamed, beginning to feel completely inadequate as her mother and telling myself I was failing because I didn't know how to make her stop. I started shutting down and telling my husband to do more to help calm her because I didn't know what to do.

I spent the first 6 weeks of her life struggling with strong and confusing emotions. I sat in the rocking chair nursing and would cry without warning, tears streaming down my face and landing on her head, wondering why I felt so awful while telling myself I wasn't a good enough mom. I was exhausted and restless and alone once our families left and my husband returned to work. I remember calling him one day and leaving a message, begging him to come home because she'd been crying for hours and I couldn't get her to stop. I would take her for walks in the stroller and she would scream the entire time – I wondered what was wrong because babies were supposed to be soothed by strolling and she wasn't. She would cry in the car and I would shut down and feel useless, so I stopped going anywhere that required more than 10 minutes of driving.

I joined a new moms support group at the birth center where I delivered her and remember sitting with this group of new moms who were well rested, happy, and calm. I was not. I cried during one group and told them I knew it would be tough and suck at times, but I didn't expect it to so soon. I felt like they thought I was crazy and had no idea what I was talking about. I felt isolated and alone and told myself I wasn't cut out for this. I started seeing a therapist at 7 months postpartum after finally admitting I was really struggling. Besides my husband, no one knew what was going on. He took the brunt of my anger, irritation, and frustration. There were days I told myself I didn't want to be a mom because I hadn't signed up for any of this. I had expectations for myself and my daughter that weren't fitting my reality and I didn't know how to handle it. My daughter was high needs and would cry every time I put her down. She rarely slept for more than 2 hours at a time. She hit all her developmental milestones early and once she became mobile at 4 months my life became infinitely more complicated. I started taking medication when she was 11 months old, and while I feel much better I continue to encounter feelings of inadequacy, failure, and unmet expectations. I'm trying to stop comparing my daughter to other babies who are not high needs and enjoy all of her great qualities, but I still struggle. I feel like I missed out on the most precious moments of her life, and I grieve for the time I won't get back. We made the decision to move back to our home state to be closer to family because I realized I needed more help and need to feel more connection to loved ones.

My daughter is almost 13 months old now, and while I can't say I've recovered, I'm on my way and feeling much better. I'm feeling optimistic and looking forward to returning to work in the next few months. I'm happy to be living closer to some dear friends, and excited she'll be able to have a relationship with her grandparents. And on the days I'm completely exhausted, worn down, and feeling defeated, I try to imagine life before her and realize my world is more complete with her in it.

Lauren and The Wolf Hour

During my doula and childbirth education days, I met a woman, Lauren who was smart, sweet, and strong. I witnessed her tenacity first hand as she pushed through and endured hours and hours of labor, completely un-medicated. When I would recommend she rest before she tuckered herself out, she continued pacing in her zone ready to persevere through another contraction. I loved her spirit and was in such admiration of her. Somehow smiling…in labor.

She began her motherhood journey with a beautiful baby girl. Many moms dreams of those hours after birth adoring the sweet bundle of joy they have been waiting nine months to see and embrace. For Lauren, something happened during pushing. Her baby was quickly separated from her due to some complications toward the end of an otherwise smooth delivery and spent four days in the NICU – (Neonatal Intensive Care Unit). Mother was recovering from some physical complications as well. She and her baby were fighters.

I met up with Lauren a few years later to talk to her about her PeriWrinkle experience. She is now a proud mom of two.

When Lauren finally made it home from the hospital with her first baby, she said that she was ready. Ready to mother. Ready to be there for her baby. She would hear every little sound and be up to tend to her baby. It became exhausting as she was unintentionally flooding herself with adrenaline. Hearing every peep. Getting up through every sound, but baby not always needing anything and momma losing sleep. By 7pm every evening she would begin to have anticipatory anxiety. She and her family referred to it as the *Wolf Hour*. She'd cry sometimes, not knowing what to expect from the night or how often she would be up. Finally, one night she stayed up and just watched her baby all night and realized – baby was fine. She was just making baby noises and being a baby. After that all-nighter, she felt a bit better and it eased some of her worries, but sleep still didn't come easy sometimes.

A big aspect of PeriWrinkle for Lauren was the stress of not wanting to make a single mistake. This tiny human was a big responsibility and being the loving mom she is, she wanted to be the best and provide the best for her daughter. She was ambitious and prepared to be a mom. Already wanting nothing less than paramount for her child. Mom wanted to read books to her baby, do tummy time, and talk to her. She felt the need to stimulate baby's brain and that it was part of her responsibility that baby meet milestones on time.

Yet, eventually she began realizing that her daughter didn't need much more stimulation beyond sleep those early days and weeks. She would talk to baby, but there wasn't much feedback initially either. No cooing or smiling much yet. Baby was just a baby. Slightly boring. There was no need to overdo it.

Lauren also felt like she needed a sense of control. This was visible with chores. She thought it perhaps came from not completely knowing what she was doing with baby or work, but she knew how to fold laundry. At that time: "Nobody can fold things the right way, or change diapers the right way except me." It gave her a sense of accomplishment.

You'll never guess what momma Lauren was doing while I was interviewing her…folding laundry. I smiled.

__Expectations__

Lauren said her expectations of maternity break were off. She did all the classes like baby basics, breastfeeding, hypnobirthing, etc. She was a straight "A" student in college, but this was different. When baby was here, in her arms, reality set in and there was a fear of breaking baby. She had her mom bathe both her babies the first time and had her mom show her even though she already knew and learned from classes. She wanted to be perfect and didn't want to accept anything less than perfection. Her children are sacred and precious to her.

She also figured she'd have a night owl partner. Company. He could sleep through baby sounds, she couldn't. She thought she'd have time to read and watch television, and have quiet moments when baby was sleeping. She said that "the whole sleeping when your baby sleeps is B.S." It just isn't as ideal and feasible as it sounds. She had hopes of relaxing and watching some television on maternity leave. That didn't happen. She was terrified of exposing her baby to screen time so she didn't watch anything. She was too afraid.

The mind before baby … the mind during PeriWrinkle. It becomes a different reality sometimes than what we thought, hoped, or expected.

She realized though that we only get these moments once and won't get that time ever again so she wanted to start enjoying it. A midwife had mentioned to her to seek help and/or try medication or something because she wouldn't want to remember this part of life in a dark way. So she did seek help and began taking medication for a little while.

What Helped:

"Family really helped. They have been there every step of the way." They were there to remind her it wasn't the end of the world, to help her calm down, and just be supportive in whatever way they could.

She also pulled together a group of other moms to meet with their babies and chocolate chip cookies. Because…yum. That sounds perfect to me. They were all a support to one another. She found that it was best to meet with moms who had infants around the same age because once they were older and mobile, it was tougher. It was a bit easier being with others in the same boat at the same time basically.

A supportive partner helped. Her husband was willing to go to any therapy appointments with her even though he could have stayed home with baby. "He was very supportive." He would tell her she was doing her best and to let baby be a ham sometimes, she didn't always need to do, do, do. "Whatever you need, WE will do."

Baby #2

Lauren was blessed with a little boy a few years later. The second time around, it was different. Still some struggles, but better. She began medication right away after her second delivery.

There were some differences the 2nd time around. Your body hurts so much the first time and you want to rest, but it's almost impossible to do so with baby AND toddler. Keeping on a schedule was helpful. Getting out of the house and doing all the things they love so much already like library trips, only now, with baby too.

She noticed the hormonal shift right away with second baby and wasn't sleeping much the first few days. She was told to practice skin-on-skin. Don't fall asleep with baby, but get naked and put baby on your chest and rock. Have someone there to make sure you don't fall asleep with baby on you, etc. She was not too sold at first, but tried it. She did skin-to-skin with second baby and said: "It was magic!"

Some Tips from Lauren

- Adjust first, then get back into your life.
  - Don't push yourself to do it all. Give yourself time to acclimate to motherhood. Example: Maybe don't go to wedding 3 weeks post-delivery while breastfeeding. Worried about breastfeeding and where and who might walk in and if the nipple shields had to be washed every time and what happens when they get lost? Having to change the baby, outside in the car, and totally worried it's too freezing cold. Too much.
- Shower
  - She highly encourages women to shower. You'll feel so much better. It was the one thing she had to do every day for herself. She didn't want her partner to leave until she got her shower and the one day he let her sleep in while he left, she was furious. "I

just needed that one thing." And to know that baby was attended to while she was in the shower.

- Don't mind what others tell you.
  - o Everyone has advice for moms. "I had arguments with my mom sometimes about how to do certain things. Sometimes just trust your gut."

It was so lovely to meet up with Lauren again. I still see that vivacious and loving essence in her. She is such a phenomenal mother with darling children.

Patricia – Mom of a Mom with PeriWrinkle – January 2019

I spoke to an exquisite lady, Patricia, who discussed some of the differences between when she was a new mom to now her role as a mother of a new mom of her grandchild.

She can remember the long hours when she first became a mom and thinking, "is she (baby) really crying again?" She remembers the typical feeling that it was more of a burden than expected. The first baby, she thought, "Oh my goodness, they just placed a baby in my hands." The internal pressure was on her to make sure this little human survived. She felt that responsibility and she owned it. She raised three beautiful children who are successful adults now.

Patricia mentioned that ignorance may have been blissful back then. They were not as aware of postpartum depression and anxiety and not inundated with all the videos like on SIDS and whatnot. Although it is great to know all the information that we know today to help save and protect babies and prevent possible tragedies, it also increases anxiety tenfold.

She saw this in her daughter. Don't do this or that. Baby can't wear jacket in the car. Baby is too warm, too cold. It's too much, not enough. Baby has to sleep this way, not that way. And so on. Patricia said it was more laid back, back then, and easier to be calm. She thinks it is harder for moms today, to just be moms and being a mom is a hard job already without lots of added pressures.

Patricia discovered that with each baby, it got easier. The first one was the toughest when you're really learning how to be a parent and all the requirements. By baby number three, she was settling more into her own rhythm as a mother and now she is bequeathing her knowledge and providing love and support to her daughter as she blossoms into motherhood.

Brendan – February 2019

I was hoping to have some input from a male as well for this book. I sent out a post and received a response from someone back in my college days. It was nice to reconnect and learn that Brendan is married to a beautiful lady and they now have a daughter together. A little rough start with a cesarean section and baby in the NICU for 48 hours, but everyone is well today.

In the early conversation, he mentioned that he received his nickname in college from his basketball coach: the "Wolf." Talk about synchronicity. I think he was meant to be a part of this book.

Brendan said his wife experienced some symptoms, but not as severe as some other people he knows. She was also taking Zoloft prior to the pregnancy as well which most likely helped. He himself was also "smacked in the face with anxiety" at age 29. He began taking antidepressant/anxiety medication for 10-11 months. His anxiety was unexpected and soon not long after it hit, his father died suddenly from a massive heart attack. Another unforeseen shock.

Life threw him into a journey, perhaps he didn't want to be on, but he now looks back with gratitude for the fact that it lead him down a spiritual path. He said he lucked out and received good support he needed.

Brendan has ambition to push through things and get to better places in his life. His experience led to a greater understanding of his wife and helped achieve a greater balance when baby arrived. Sure, there are some parenting discrepancies that were challenging at first, just different male/female mentalities in general, but a learning process they have done together.

It was wonderful catching up with Brendan. I am grateful to him for sharing his story and happy he is a testament to others that there is hope beyond anxiety. His contribution to this book has provided me with some great tips that perhaps might be of help to you.

<u>Advice</u>

1. Find a good doctor who is understanding, cares, and listens.
2. Medication – it is available and helps and he says to use as a crutch not a cure or solution.
3. Find a therapist that works for you and is a good fit. He also found a yoga instructor/therapist that was very helpful.
4. Have a good support team and outside of the family or close friend group. People who are neutral and won't judge.
5. He says there is a light at the end of the tunnel. You can do this.
6. What works for me might not work for you. Find what works for you.

7. Some of the following were things that he learned and were very beneficial to him and now he helps others learn some of these:
    a. Meditation
    b. Tai Chi – "meditation in motion"/form of Chinese martial arts
    c. Reiki – alternative energy healing

Author – Susie

Although long, my delivery was "Best Day Ever." I started having contractions the night before and the next day I went for a hike, hoping gravity would expedite labor. Later at home, a movie, cards, and family helped pass the time and distract me from labor. When things began to progress, I was really starting to feel it, and the contractions were stronger, longer, and closer together, I called The Midwife Center. It was about an hour north from where I lived so I wanted to make sure I had time to get there. Little did I know, I would still have another twelve hours to go, but I felt more relief in knowing I'd be there verses on the road delivering a baby.

After the 28 hours I spent at home laboring, I arrived at the midwife center around midnight on June 5th and occupied the Ocean Room. It was so serene and calming. Shades of blue and some nautical décor. I had a doula, Nicole. Being a doula myself, I knew the benefits and my husband at the time, Steve, had also acquired a sports injury prior to due date and would need a donor ACL and meniscal repairs. I figured a doula might be helpful for him too. Our family waited and waited and waited upstairs in the waiting area. What troupers they were. Anticipating the birth of the very first grandchild on both sides.

I wanted an un-medicated and completely natural childbirth, not to prove anything as far as pain goes, but rather because I knew I couldn't be tied down in bed and I wanted a healthy experience for me and my child. I understood the possibilities of perhaps needing a cesarean section or needing Pitocin, which would have probably resulted in me needing an epidural. I was a doula. I knew all the unknowns, the complications that could arise, but I was ready to see if me and my baby could do this on our own together as a team.

I came prepared with my bag of goodies. A tennis ball – excellent for lower back massage. Other massage tools, our wedding music on a CD, camera, baby's first outfit to go home after birth.

Contractions hurt. In between the contractions, it was lovely and I could interact and laugh and enjoy the day. It was a very special moment in my life and a special time for Steve and me. Despite his knee injury, he didn't leave my side. He was supportive and loving and was exactly what I needed in that moment of my life. I was about to become a momma and I couldn't wait to meet my daughter finally. We couldn't wait to meet our first child, and finally reveal her name to everyone.

I spent a lot of time in the Jacuzzi tub. I called it my "Aquadural" instead of Epidural. My water didn't break at all and when I was 10 centimeters fully dilated, I was offered the choice to push with the amniotic sac intact. Although I thought it would be neat to see, I think I was just ready to move things along and meet my little girl. So, the midwife pulled out an amnihook and before I knew it, it was go time.

Pushing took longer than expected. A long time actually, but it was worth the wait and exhaustion. It was love at first sight. I held her and never wanted to let go. I was happy that the midwife staff did most of their exams/assessments with my beautiful Skyla Rose in my arms, on my belly, and/or in the bed beside me. Steve behind me, holding me. The three of us in a warm embrace. It couldn't have been more perfect. Well, except the "zoo" part. They only allowed our family and friends initially (even the ones who drove from out of state) to just come look at baby. I felt like the three of us were on display at a zoo. I didn't like that moment. I wanted our family, who had been there, waiting long hours with us, to come and interact awhile. Looking back, I regret not saying anything and pushing for what I wanted.

I left to go home a few hours later. Naturally sore, but I was feeling pretty good. At home, the visitors came and went. Immense joy filled me as each one got to meet and hold her for the first time. I savored all that love our sweet baby was blessed with. Watching the faces of family and friends as they got lost in a loving gaze, brought joy to my heart.

I couldn't take my eyes off of my baby. I never knew you could stare at something so lovingly for so long, but only feel like a minute had passed. I got lost in the awe of this miracle in my arms. There was a new light in my life and I felt so very blessed.

That light, however, gradually began to dim. So gradual, I could barely tell that the bulb needed changed. It became dimmer and dimmer, until one day, it burned out. I found myself fumbling in the dark. Pretending that my world was still in HD, bright and crystal clear.

Breast feeding proved to be challenging. I wanted to do it. I knew it was healthy for baby and me in so many ways. I had a nurse try telling me not to do it because of my breast reduction. "What was wrong with her?" I thought. She put me down and made me feel awful for not giving my baby enough that first day. I work in the field. I knew that all she needed was a few drops of colostrum and that her belly was the size of a marble. This was probably the beginning of the joy of new motherhood fading.

My baby was a picky and fussy eater. She was so energetic she would move too much and push herself off. Then she would be fussy because she was hungry. She was not a good sleeper initially. It was not easy like the class video. I became tired and worn out and emotionally spent from not sleeping and constantly trying to feed and pump.

The nurses would call to check-in. "I'm great!" I would tell them and I was fine the first few weeks, but then I wasn't, but I couldn't tell them that. "What if they think I'm a bad mom for not being perfect for my child? What if they take her away? What if they think I suck at new mother-hood?" What if, what if, what if!!! The lies of "I'm Fine," protected me from anyone possibly thinking I was anything less than the absolute best and perfect mom in the world. If anyone saw even a minimal flaw – I was a failure. Already labeled in my head, and just one notion from an outside source would confirm this belief. The nurse asked again,

"Are you sure you're okay?" "Yes. Baby is growing and wonderful." Deflect.

Yet, within, anxiety flooded me. I worried about whether my baby was breathing when she was sleeping. I worried about whether I was feeding her right and enough. I worried about germs and started going through bottles of hand sanitizer. I worried about what other people thought of me as a mom. I worried, worried, worried. I couldn't just be, just exist, just relax and enjoy motherhood. Steve had his knee surgery soon after and I remember when his family visited, all I could think about was "What if they think I am not doing enough? What if they think I'm a bad wife?" I was healing after labor, caring for a newborn, breastfeeding, pumping and sweetly caring for his wounds and getting him food and filling the ice-cooler attached to his leg. The gal who just spent forty hours in labor, didn't think she was doing enough. In actuality – I was doing too much.

No one ever told me about the anxiety that could creep up. I knew about postpartum depression. I knew deep down that it was starting to infiltrate my life, but I didn't know that anxiety was doing the same. It all came on so slowly, I didn't recognize the changes happening to me and I wanted to stay in denial. Denial, though, just led to feeling worse. I didn't want to die, but there were definite moments when I couldn't fathom facing another day. Because living with PeriWrinkle was its own kind of hell.

On one hand, I was telling myself that my beautiful, sweet baby would be better off with someone else, not someone as anxious and down like me. On the other hand, I was telling myself that no one could love her and protect her as well as I could and give her what she needs. Yet, still on the other hand, I was telling myself that I didn't deserve her. It was madness. An off-tune chorus of rapidly intrusive thoughts clouding my head. Rationally, I knew all this was false. Huge cognitive distortions. Negative thoughts like popcorn popping into my mind. But I should know better, right? I should have a better handle on it, right? I should just stop the thoughts, right? Just get over it, right? I just had the best child birth experience I could have ever imagined; I have no reason to be feeling crappy after.

My color was fading as fast as my light did, but no one could know. So, I just painted on some temporary colors, but that only worked until they kept washing off. So much that I became convinced that I was going to have to change careers after maternity leave. How could I be a counselor and help people if I couldn't even help myself? My world was falling apart. At least it felt that way at the time. I started looking up new jobs. I considered a job at a zoo because animals wouldn't care whether or not I couldn't stop the rat race in my monkey mind.

Peri-freakin'-wrinkle. My nurses calling to check on me, missed it. My doctor at the time, however, she was on it. She saw right through. I am forever grateful to Dr. Andrews. She looked me in the eyes and asked me again if I was okay. I broke down in her office in tears. She was a blessing. No judgement. Just pure sympathy and information to help me reach out for additional services. She told me of moments she had as a new mom. That helped more than anything. If my doc had similar feelings and experiences once and she is here standing AND I think she is an extraordinary human being, I'd be okay.

I went to a counselor who was sweet and kind, but I didn't feel I could confide in her and I wasn't getting what I needed. She showed me a poem and wanted to know what I thought. I didn't care about poems or articles or anything at that point in time. "You should exercise. It helps depression." Um…but I'm four weeks postpartum and can't until at least my six week OB check-up, if all is okay. I wanted real help for my situation, not just any anxiety/depression. I tried another therapist. "Well, you're a therapist. You know what to do." But what I wanted and needed then was to be the patient. Just a few sessions in, she showed up a half hour late for my appointment, but charged me for a full hour session. I should have taken action then, but how could I when I was fighting just to survive every day? What it did teach me though, was what not to do as a therapist! It also taught me to tell others to not give up. Keep searching. You have to find the right fit for you and get the help you need. Most people find the right fit the first time. I think I didn't because in retrospect, it was part of my life/career journey.

Flash forward to now, I can say it all propelled me to be a much, much better therapist than I could have imagined. Because now, I get it! I can empathize. I am not perfect by any means, but hope to always do the best I can, knowing personally how tough that wrinkle in perinatal time was.

You help better and more authentically when you've been in the trenches and come out alive. I realized I didn't know as much as I thought about helping women with postpartum until after my experience. Perhaps it was one of the reasons I went through it – to help other women. I knew what worked for me and what didn't and I could offer more suggestions. I didn't self-disclose to everyone, usually only if they asked, but it was a relief to so many to know there was hope. That even their therapist wasn't immune from PeriWrinkle.

After that second failed attempt for help, something just clicked. And thank God. I knew I had to get better. My child needed me and I didn't want other women to go through what I did. What I didn't get, I wanted to give. What I desperately wanted, someone out there was waiting to receive. I talked to my doc again and she started me on Zoloft. Six months on it was like a perfect reset for me.

There are still gaps that need worked on in the system all around…as discussed in chapter thirteen as well as women who have to stay inpatient being separated from their infants. Things aren't perfect. We live in an imperfect world, but things are always improving. So, please, be your own best advocate too and if you aren't feeling up to it, have your partner or someone else help speak up with you and for you. Don't give up. Along this journey I have met more and more amazing workers in this field. Treatment is getting better and more advanced. Education and screening is helping to catch it sooner. Word is getting out there and women don't have to suffer alone anymore.

Years later, when my little one was five, I attempted to find a therapist again. Apprehensive after my previous experience, but in need. My dad recently died from leukemia and I was in the midst of a separation. I found a therapist and she was everything I needed and more than I could have wished for. Elana was a perfect fit and a phenomenal person. She was helpful and knowledgeable. Nonjudgmental and there was a level of comfort and ease. She became a part of colossal growth in my life. Yes, even therapists benefit from therapy at times. Find your person and grow baby grow.

Inside a PeriWrinkled Mind

(A Segment of Thoughts and Reflections from Within Minds of Women during PeriWrinkle)

Swirling Thoughts

Night has fallen and the only sound I hear ... not crickets ... but the thoughts in my head.

They swirl and loop on repeat.

The feeling-after hangover.

A dark and dreary state.

So heavy my body can't lift itself out of bed. Head too heavy, it doesn't leave the pillow. But it has to. I hear the cries. I must get up.

I get up. I put on a smile. The smile I wish was real for my baby. I want to be happy. I wanted my baby. If my mind won't let me be happy, I'm still going to fake it and lift the corners of my lips because she deserves that.

Why can't I be like every other mother who doesn't have to experience this? How can I even tell anyone that something is wrong? They'll think I'm a horrible mom. A horrible person. I wish I could control it. I desperately want to be happy and feel normal again. The others are all so perfect and handle it all. I can barely get through a day. It doesn't seem fair. I don't wish this on anyone. I'm happy that they are happy, but I want that too.

<u>Inside a PeriWrinkled Mind</u>

<u>Losing Yourself</u>

I tried to fight it.

But without much sleep at all…

My own 24/7 milk factory…

Hormonal Fluctuations…

It took over.

Before I knew it.

I didn't even feel like me anymore.

<u>Portal</u>

Sucked into a portal of swirling darkness. An easy entry but I can't find the exit anywhere. No one will help me. I'm trying to help myself, but there is nothing to hold on to. Spinning and spinning. Dizzy. Falling. Failing.

"Snap out of it."

I'm trying. Don't you get it? It's not working. I wish it did because an easy fix like that would be worth more than gold.

<u>Mean Girls</u>

Guilt. Shame. Low Self-Worth.

Mean Girls in my head.

When rational thoughts are caged and locked.

They are there…but unobtainable.

At least…they feel out of reach.

<u>No One Cares</u>

A sometimes harsh reality.

Sometimes it seems that no one cares or notices when you pull away. Their lives go on. No one stops to ask where you've been. How ya doing? No one knows what to say, so they say nothing at all.

Something depression will do to you is make you withdraw. No energy for your usual social activities. And anxiety will make you worry what they think anyway.

This just exacerbates the loneliness and withdraw.

And if you're a self-critical, but "kind to everyone else" depressive, then you're too worried about others…no one wants to be around a sad person. What if I accidentally mess up their day or life? I can't spread misery on others. Just leave them alone to be happy the way they are.

Go mute. The less you say, the less anyone can hold against you.

A vicious cycle, going nowhere but down.

Don't listen to the lies of your brain and even when it feels no one is there for you:

Sometimes you have to pick yourself up and carry-on.

There will be earth angels along the way to keep you going if you are open to seeing and receiving.

But get up first, they will find you. It might not be who you expected either.

Be receptive and reach out when necessary.

You Can Do This! I have faith in you. You are stronger than you know.

Befriend Yourself

So, sometimes, you have to be your own best advocate and friend.

Not everyone will know what to do or say when it comes to PeriWrinkle stuff.

I know, your eyes are bulging and you are probably mumbling, "WTH? Why do I have to be the one to love me?"

Because we all know we are our own worst enemy and you might not feel like you have the energy. But kicking yourself when you're down won't help either.

Lift yourself up. Even if just a little a day.

Don't wanna?

But do it anyway!

We don't have to be our enemy.

Befriend yourself. Be kind to you.

With Depression, Everyday Can Be Hard

It is crazy – depression. When it takes over, even the things you would normally think would give you enough reasons to live, depression tells you why those reasons are not legit. It de-rationalizes worth and meaning in life. It turns the beauty of motherhood into – "my baby deserves better than me." Someone else could support my baby financially. No one else could love my baby like me, but I don't want my baby to have to grow up with a mom who gets depressed, even though I try to hide it…I know one day my baby will know and will walk away like everyone else. No one wants to be around someone who is down. Everyone else is weeding their pretty little gardens with no room for friends or family with mental illness.

With depression, every day can be hard. The pain – you just learn to walk with it. Carry it with you…EVERY single day. Every single day. I carry the fear. Fear of tomorrow. The unknown. I don't want to struggle forever. I don't want my emotions to always feel so tough and unwanted. I don't want to cry all the time. I don't want to feel numb.

Remember, this is temporary. Freedom comes when you seek help and learn to let go of these strong grips of depression and anxiety. It will be a feather feeling when you get to the place of wanting to ditch the heavy black clouds and carry a smile on your face. Not every day in life will be perfect, but not every day has to be or feel like a struggle.

Anxiety

An invisible hand permeated the barriers of my skin and chest wall.

Gripping my heart so tight, breathlessness took over. On the brink of a panic attack.

To stay in control. To muscle through. Pull myself together.

Deep slow breaths. Fighting it will surely cause the hand to continue squeezing my heart like a stress ball.

Release its grasp. I envision being freed. I envision my heart growing so large and in charge, it breaks the chains. It opens my lungs. I stand tall. Power posing. Breathing in energy and strength.

Exhaling relief and release.

Climbing out of the Darkness

Then the storm clouds move in and take away your sunshine. You didn't ask for it. You don't welcome it. But it's there. Dark and bleak and ominous and thunders a might roar over you, strikes you with a painful electric blast and soaks you in a downpour of negative emotions.

I've let life knock me down.

I sat in and with the pain.

Embraced it.

Just about every second of it, dreadful.

Somehow, someway, I came out of the darkness. I can't remember if I crawled, or climbed, or fumbled, but I found the light.

It doesn't make sense to be in the darkness in the first place. Not when it's supposed to be the happiest time of your life. The moment you planned for, spent 9 months anticipating, what he/she will look like.

You envision your child in the adorable outfits you have picked out in advance. You are already looking forward to kindergarten and high school graduation. Proms, wedding, career and who knows what else. All sorts of hopes and dreams.

If you had fertility issues – wanted even more and so grateful for your blessing, you really don't want to be down after all you went through to conceive. Even harder to understand the darkness.

But darkness doesn't exist without light. Crawl, climb, fall, get back up, adjust your sails, stumble… do whatever. Just keep moving. The sun returns once the moon falls asleep.

<u>Shades of PeriWrinkle Light</u>

And suddenly a ray of light broke through.

Like sunshine bursting through a cloud.

Darkness was disintegrating.

Fog was lifting.

Chains released from my wrists.

That one ray of sun melted the chill that had settled in my soul.

I could breathe again.

I felt like me again.

I could dance again.

The world was beautiful once more.

<u>Part III: Grow Me</u>

<u>Introduction</u>

This segment of the book is a compilation of tools, insights, self-help, and inspirational quotes to help you along your PeriWrinkle journey. May we never stop growing and learning.

A Dash of Self-Help and a Sprinkle of Self-Care

When I was struggling with PeriWrinkle, I read the books that were either basically a biography - *Here's my story*. Great, you sound somewhat like me. Or the ones where there was a ton of information about what it is, but none of them helped me with what I needed to do. I remember thinking, "Ok, so I know I don't feel myself and I just spent a ton of time reading … just to confirm what I already know." Now what though? I found very little tips or advice at that time. I was reading the stories of women when they were in it, but not of the other side. I needed hope and light, even if I couldn't see it yet.

I hope this helps you not just confirm that what you're going through is real and happens to other people and you are not alone; also that there is hope and help available and you can start here with a few tips. Of course, everyone is individually beautiful and unique. Some things work for some women and other things just don't cut it. Find what works for you.

So, I wanted to give you a few tools at least to get started, but please, if you are reading this and need help, go seek medical treatment as well. We have advanced and there are some great therapists and/or psychiatrists out there to help you. You don't have to suffer alone and you deserve the most comprehensive care you and baby can get. Every mother deserves to enjoy her pregnancy and postpartum.

On the next few pages, I'll provide individual tools you can do at home. Some of these can also be found in my eBook on Amazon.com: *"Swimming in a Sea of Octopuses: Adapting to Increasing Speeds of Life."*

❖ **SLEEP** – best medicine for a mom – block of 6 hours a night. Otherwise, there is no down time for her neurotransmitters to heal. Even meds won't work if you're not sleeping. Try to have at least 30 min wind down time. No electronics. Take a hot bath/shower, try essential oils (lavender, lemon grass), relaxation, guided imagery, read book in chair then hop right in bed (bed for sleep and sexy time only), protein snack before bed like eggs so your sugar won't drop at night and wake you up hangry. Epsom salts help relax muscles, and decrease twitching and irritability.

❖ **Immerse yourself in something greater than yourself** – This was something that specifically helped me. Go to a waterfall. It drowns out thoughts; so powerful. Watch a Sunrise or Sunset. Meditate at a lake. Experience awe-inspiring moments. Get lost in the magic of nature.

❖ **Relaxation Exercises** – Try yoga. Deep breathing. Hot bath.

❖ **Exercise** – when appropriate after physical recovery. Even if just going for a stroll. Ten jumping jacks and if that makes you tinkle after giving birth, then some low key things like abdominal exercises, stretching, swimming, weights, … whatever works for you.

❖ **Social Network** – even if you hang out with just one friend. Quality is better than quantity and you need people. Even if you think you don't and would prefer to withdraw. It's a biological fact. Connection is huge.

- ❖ **Grounding Skills** – use all five senses to keep you in the present moment. It can help re-orient you to right now when you are becoming anxious, overwhelmed, and too stressed and get you out of your head when those thoughts are tripping in the future or trying to post #tbt – throwback Thursdays. Nope, right here. Right now.
- ❖ **Shake out those stuffy feelings** – Healthy ways include talking and journaling.
- ❖ **Light Therapy** – go outside for some sunshine. If it is winter and dark where you are, try a light therapy box. You can order online or check with your doctor.
- ❖ **Massages and/or Acupuncture**
- ❖ **Support Groups**
- ❖ **Psychotherapy**
- ❖ **Lower Expectations** – you don't have to be Super Mom or Mom of the Year.
- ❖ **Skip housework**. Make yourself and baby a priority. The other stuff will get back on track eventually.
- ❖ **Meditation** – Even just a few minutes a day and if you're not sure how. Check out apps like *Insight Timer*.
- ❖ **Nutrition** – bottom line, your body needs fuel and the best possible kind.
- ❖ **Stay Hydrated** – be a mermaid and consume lots of water. Fresh, not salty.
- ❖ **Read** – particularly uplifting books and informative ones on postpartum mood and anxiety disorders. Read fiction novels to have a break and relax. Read to your baby.

- **Soul Food** – when feeling down, try focusing on the things that bring you joy and uplifts you.
- **Ask for Help**
- **Be Receptive to Help**
- **Flexibility** - Know that there will be some good days and some not so good days. And good and bad moments in each day.
- **Take One Day at a Time**
- **Faith. Religion.**
- **Smile** – even if you don't feel like it. Your brain might respond. Watch your baby smile and smile back. It will cause fireworks in your brain. Not really, but it will stimulate areas to create a natural high.
- **Sing** – I actually heard on the radio heading to work one day that singing can activate a pleasure center in the brain. I find it just to be soothing when I'm in the car or shower.
- **Dance** – no one has to watch.
- **Consider Medication** – time for a visit with your doc.
- **Draw. Adult Coloring Books. Mandalas**
- **Take time for yourself. Pamper yourself**
- **Yet!** – I like to add this to the end of statements (usually negative ones). For example: "I can't get the hang of this mothering thing…YET!" "Since baby was born, I haven't even been able to wear anything besides my pajamas…YET!" "I don't fully love myself…YET!"
- **Self-Love** - If you catch yourself being hard on yourself – Stop. Take a deep breath. Tell yourself something kind. Even if you don't feel like the most amazing person right now you can still be kind to

yourself. Find a gentler approach. You can say things like:

- o   You are doing the best you can.
- o   You got up today. That's better than yesterday.
- o   You just cleaned up puke and a dirty diaper. You deserve your own sticker chart…the scratch-and-sniff cool kinds.
- o   You didn't accidentally squirt the dog with breast milk today. Score!
- o   You are worthy of love.
- o   You work so hard and do so much. Just feeding your baby is an amazing task.
- o   You are not alone.
- o   It's okay to feel scared, stressed, frustrated…
- o   It's okay to cry.
- o   It's okay to rest.
- o   You can now win a shower marathon. It used to take you an hour. Now you can pee, shower and dress in like 10 minute flat.
- o   You have one sock on today. That's better than none.
- o   You lost zero pacifiers today. Phew. You rock.
- o   Everyone makes mistakes. Perfection is an illusion.
- o   You got this!
- o   I am learning and growing every day.
- o   I belong and I am good enough just the way I am.

<u>An extra dash of sprinkled advice:</u>

Your doc might give you an assessment test. Most likely it'll be The Edinburg Postnatal Depression Screening Scale or the Postpartum Depression Screening Scale. My advice to you is to answer it as honestly as possible. I wanted to answer the questions with how I wanted to feel and with answers I wanted my doctor to see. I wanted her to think I was fine and dandy. I didn't want her to think I was struggling. What if she thought I was a bad mom? Okay, but I wasn't going to get any help if I kept leading on that I was perfect and wonderful. These screening tools are meant to gage where you are and get the best help for you possible. As professionals, we want to meet you where you are so we can help you on that journey to get to where you want to be.

It might be worth also having your vitamin/mineral levels checked as well as your thyroid.

Oh, and just to be extra because I think you deserve it…there's plenty more if you keep turning the page or swiping the screen.

So, You Want to Lick a Salt Lamp?

I am a therapist and I pride myself in trying to maintain as much focus as possible in my sessions as I believe the people sitting across from me deserve such respect.

However, there was that one day… and that one day eventually became therapeutic. The day I bought a salt lamp and put in my office. During a session, I was intently listening until the glowing lamp in the corner of my office put me in a trance and called to me, "Lick Me." What? "You know you want to." Okay, it didn't talk to me, but this automatic thought popped into my head. Curiosity like a cat, had me wondering if a Himalayan Salt Lamp actually tasted like salt. I can only assume. Yes, I am still wondering…and if you're wondering…I, of course … quickly refocused my attention back on session. No, I didn't lick it.

That thought was an easy one to see, observe momentarily, and then, let it go. A funny one. If only all thoughts were this easy to release and if only they could be humorous enough that if you couldn't let go for a moment, you could at least feel good while thinking it. But easy, funny, or not, they are all, after all, just thoughts, that can be released. Even the negative and scary ones.

When things just pop into your head quickly like that, they are referred to as: Automatic Thoughts. When they are unpleasant, unwanted, and often repetitive, we call these: ANTS (Automatic Negative Thoughts) or Intrusive Thoughts.

There is a difference between thoughts and action. You can have a thought like *"Lick a Salt Lamp,"* but you then have the ability to choose whether or not you act upon that thought. If you struggle with Impulse Control, then you may lack that ability and lick the lamp anyway.

It is one thing to have an impulse control issue, but if this isn't you, then you can tell yourself that your thoughts are just thoughts and nothing more. Send them to "the cloud." I never know where things go in the "cloud." I can never find it again. Send your thoughts there.

A few months after I had this salt-licking thought, my daughter was visiting and when I walked into my office, there she stood. The soft, peach glow of the Himalayan lamp, illuminating her youthful face with a warm, amber luminosity. Her tongue, completely in contact with the salty statue on my desk. I laughed, yes, out loud, and had to ask.

"What?" she responded, "I just wanted to see if it tasted like salt." Of course she did. And of course at her age, there is nothing wrong in her mind with scientifically testing out her theory. As far as social acceptability and couth as a grown-up…I suggest sticking with impulse control.

We all have automatic, intrusive thoughts. Some are pleasant, some are weird, and some are terrifying. Our brain is just wired that way. We might spend a lot of time fighting them, wishing them away, deflecting, ignoring, etc. But remember:

Lastly for this Thoughtful Chapter of Salt-Licking Salty Thoughts:

Don't believe everything you think.

You are not your thoughts.

Catch a Healthy Thought

A thought occurred to me when I thought of the parenting technique of "catch 'em being good." During a moment in session I interrupted a young lady when I heard a healthy and empowering statement. It had been awhile in the midst of current, difficult situations she was facing. I gave her a high five and then I had her repeat it. Her face softened. A smile lifted.

Thoughts are powerful things. If you were to think of the saddest moment of your life right now, your body would respond to that thought. Your face would droop, body sulk, and perhaps you might cry. But it is just a thought. It is not actually occurring right now. If I asked you to think of the happiest moment of your life and tell me about it. I would see your face light up, the corners of your lips raise, you might sit up straighter. Again, it is just a thought. A recall. It isn't happening now. That is the Power of a Thought. It can even make your body respond within nanoseconds.

Think of the good you could do when you catch a health thought and let it simmer and just savor it and let the effects wash over your entire being.

Therapists: Interrupt the session when you hear a good thought, point out the moment, repeat, praise….make it stand out and be memorable. Immerse in positive emotions.

I like gratitude journals for similar reasons, attitudes and actions of gratitude. It reiterates upon the good and grows beautiful flowers in our mind.

Activity: _Thought Catching Jar_

At home, keep a jar handy, decorate if desired, and label it: _Thought Catching Jar_.

When you hear yourself say or when you are thinking a good thought…write it down and put it in the jar. (If your partner, friends, or family hear you say one – they too can write it and put it in the jar.)

Increases awareness.

Repetition – building stronger neural pathways

A lovely reminder to have to go back and read later and smile.

Gratitude Journal

Developing an attitude of gratitude as they say is really and truly a great, if not one of the best, defenses to have against unwanted negative emotions. Psychologist reveal that when you think about what you appreciate, it boosts your level of happiness and overall well-being. Journaling these moments will have an even greater impact as you will be connecting more neurons and sparking greater awareness to not only remember the good aspects of every day, but also recognizing more good that is surrounding you every single day. There is beauty everywhere, IF you are looking for it.

I challenge you to write something different every day. It doesn't work if your daily gratitude journal is "I woke up again today." If I had the same one daily, I would just write down my daughter's name because she is the biggest blessing in my life. Challenge your mind and really look for new and inspiring things and the things that you really appreciate. When you look for the good and pay attention to positives, even if tiny, you train your mind to see more of it.

Be sure to actually write it down too, not just think about it in your head as the act of writing appreciations will produce more glitter in your mind.

Don't have time as a parent??? Try incorporating the awesome skills you wish to be doing, with your kiddos. Age appropriate of course. An infant will not be able to do physically do a gratitude journal with you, but why not talk to them about what you are writing and help them build vocabulary and learn positivity early in life. By age 3 or 4, they might be able to start drawing something that makes them happy and by grade school, they can write down something they are grateful for every day. It could be a family event. Ten minutes in the morning or before bed. Or some sort of self-care regimen. Completely up to you. Just suggestions.

Practice more appreciation and look around for it. The more you look for it, the more you will find. Notice the feeling you get inside you when this happens. Warm fuzzies. Ooey Gooey Warm Fuzzies!

<u>Grow Me – From Yours Truly, Susie</u>

- Postpartum depression and anxiety may think it's burying you…but it doesn't know you are a seed.
- Blossom my friend.
- No matter how tiny, progress is still progress.
- Close your eyes.
- Take a breath.
- Inhale calmness.
- Exhale Stress.
- Make a Cuppa.
- Savor the Aroma.
- Sip and Relax.
- It will all be okay.
- Something took over. Find your fight again.
- Even as a broken crayon, I could still color.
- If PeriWrinkle lies and says you're broken or damaged…
  - Stand tall and speak the truth and remind it that you are:
    - Growing, Healing, and Worthy of Goodness and Sparkling Moments
- Get up
- Dress up
- Go out
- Get your shine on
- Self-Care
- You've got to Nourish to Flourish

<u>Floating</u>

An alternative coping skill and/or stress management activity that I have not seen in other postpartum books…Floating. It was never something I was privy to when going through my PeriWrinkle issues. I offer this insight to you as I recently discovered floating and love it. No, it's not for everyone, but for some people it is a great way to decrease stress, anxiety, depression and to take time to relax, self-reflect, and practice mindfulness. It can even be great during pregnancy. Of course, check with your doctor first.

So, what it is?

It is literally a tank or a pod that is filled with a little bit of water (10 inches) and a whole lot of salt. Like 1,200 pounds of Epsom Salt. This type of salt was discovered in Epsom, England. It is a mineral compound of magnesium and sulfate that looks like table salt. It is known to be a natural exfoliant with anti-inflammatory properties.

The water in the tank will match your body temperature. You will have to shower before getting in the tank. It will not be as warm as a hot tub. The reason it will coincide with your body temperature is so that you won't feel it. Sensory Deprivation.

It is sound proof and will be pitch black once you enter. (However, some place do offer options of different colored lights). There are disposable earplugs to drown out sound. I recommend that you definitely wear these, not just to deplete sound, but also so you aren't left with salt water and crystals in your ears for days after.

Then…you float, effortlessly, in darkness, for whatever time you choose. Most people opt for a 60 or 90 minute session.

Floating is said to have beneficial effects on mood, blood pressure and decrease levels of the stress hormone cortisol.

For more detailed information on floating, the experience, and tips, check out my book: *"Diving into the Void: Sensory Deprivation Tank."*

Try floating your way to peace and contentment. Float your worries away.

Mom Self-Care 101

You may have heard the many cliché phrases like "you can't pour from an empty cup" or that you have to put your oxygen mask on first in order to help save others. Well, they are true and there is reason they exist. Self-care is essential.

What is it? I know this word seems to have gained popularity in recent years. I think for good reason. We need it! We say we need it a lot, but we don't actually do it.

If you don't know how, start by looking at what it is you want/need in life and do that. The gist of **Self-Care** is that it is a deliberate act of taking care of **You-Sweet-You**. It is very individualized aimed at achieving an over-all sense of well-being and inner peace. What might work for me might not work for you. One person might want to add "Drink more water" to their self-care plan but someone else may already stay plenty hydrated day to day but need better sleep habits instead.

When you think of self-care, first look at your deficits and then create a plan that will help you take better care of you. Be sure to take a look at and include multiple avenues such as:

- Physical - nutrition, exercise, medical care, sleep
- Mental - journal, relax, write down positive quotes
- Emotional - support network, counseling
- Spiritual - prayer, meditation, nature

- Intellectual – reading, learning something new, take a class

Also consider all of this in regards to the following realms of your life:

- Personal
- Professional
- Relationships

These are just a few examples. What is lacking in your life that you would like to change? In what ways could you be taking better care of you so as to be more effective and productive to others? Remember YOUR self-care plan is meant to benefit YOUR well-being. You don't want to create a plan that is so overwhelming that it creates more stress and or makes you not want to do it. The purpose is to help you feel better and be able to live at your best capacity.

Also, once you have created a self-care plan, don't forget to put that plan into action. Prioritize it and remember: **"You Are Important!"**

<u>List of Self-Care Tips</u>

From: <u>https://theselfcompassionproject.com/2013/06/03/80-self-care-ideas/</u>

1. going for a photo walk
2. going to the forest
3. a bath at the end of the day
4. going for bike rides
5. finding overgrown grass and putting my bare feet and it
6. lying in the grass on the hill and staring up at the sky
7. cooking a meal for myself and being really present
8. getting up early and reading inspirational books
9. journaling
10. walking with my dogs
11. nature
12. going places–getting a change of scenery
13. trying new things in general
14. guided meditation
15. listening to books and music
16. face-to-face conversations with people
17. gratitude journal
18. better diet
19. trying to live more authentically
20. not skipping sleep to get things done
21. trying to multitask less
22. scheduling time to myself every day
23. reading blogs from people who are honest
24. reading for pleasure
25. resting with my cat a few feet away
26. yoga
27. running
28. getting my hair done
29. getting a manicure
30. baking
31. hiding
32. knitting

33. crocheting
34. spinning
35. online classes
36. just for fun novels
37. crafting
38. being able to set limits for myself
39. asking for what I need
40. taking time for slow contemplative morning coffee
41. cuddling with my cats
42. taking my vitamins
43. burning candles
44. waking up naturally–no alarm clock
45. eating when I feel like it–not by the clock
46. eating a fresh bagel at a local shop while doing a crossword puzzle
47. chocolate
48. daily stretching
49. good movies
50. getting massages
51. working with a life coach
52. prayer
53. paying attention to my breathing
54. gathering flowers from my garden
55. planting flowers in my garden for later gathering
56. art journaling
57. stealing a few moments to lie on my bed when the afternoon sun is streaming in through the window
58. coffee at coffee shops
59. centering prayer
60. mindfulness
61. forgiveness of others so I don't carry that stuff around
62. simplifying
63. a glass of wine at the end of the day
64. fresh air
65. eclectic playlists
66. live music
67. book club

68. support groups
69. creating a comfortable house that truly is my home
70. cuddling with my puppies
71. taking myself out to eat
72. move my body–dance, exercise, run
73. dress up in the way I want to feel
74. taking action
75. laughter
76. tears
77. hot shower
78. giving back with my time
79. being a tourist in my own city
80. lunch dates with good friends
81. green smoothies
82. take painkillers when I need to instead of holding out and suffering
83. learn to be with and accept my feelings
84. have adventures and drive to new places
85. spend less time on the Internet
86. read the newspaper on Sundays at a café
87. read poetry or inspiring quotes
88. volunteering
89. attending church

And if that wasn't enough, here is a great website with 134 Self-Care Activities:
http://www.goodtherapy.org/blog/134-activities-to-add-to-your-self-care-plan/

<u>Reality Check</u>

"What screws us up most in life is the picture in our head of how it's supposed to be." ~Jeremy Binns

Especially if this is your first baby, prepare for reality checks. I was pregnant and on cloud nine preparing the nursery. Every dresser drawer had perfectly folded burp cloths, socks, blankets, etc. Everything in its place. Darling onesies and outfits hung just so in the closet in order from newborn up to the largest size I had.

This was about to be the best time in my life. I was ready.

Haha! Reality…

Insecurities about parenting abilities.

Establishing feeding practices. Not on a schedule. On a schedule. Schedule is all messed up again.

Loss of freedom. Feeling tied down.

Loss of old identity.

Body image changes.

Self-esteem may go on a downward slope.

Financial differences.

Shaken career path or identity or potential.

Scheduled sex. Penciled in, erased, penciled again. Hubby wants spontaneity. Baby starts crying in the next room during foreplay. Where'd sex go?

Put on brand new, darling outfit. Blow out diaper within seconds. Put baby in whatever you can find that's left and isn't in the washer.

. . . .

. . . .

. . . .

. . . .

. . . .

. . . .

. . . .

. . . .

. . . .

. . . .

. . . .

Insert your reality checks above.

Positive Affirmations

Screw that Shit.

Surprised I said that? Me too, but here's why…

As a rookie therapist way back in the days when I still lived in Maryland, I would tell people about Positive Affirmations. That is what you learn in college. Tell people to write down positive things about themselves on sticky notes and put on their mirror or somewhere they'll see it every day. Okay, great concept, **IF** you're feeling pretty good already. **IF** you're motivated enough and not in the midst of perinatal hormones. I quickly realized that I was about to chuck this from my therapy skills list. What did I do with those sticky notes during postpartum? I ripped them to shreds. They angered me because I didn't feel that way. Because I so badly wanted to feel that way, but was struggling to get there, and because I used to feel that way, but it was taken from me. I hated those stupid positive notes of affirmation. Screw them, I said.

Is positivity important? Absolutely and I do it all the time…now. I love working with clients from a positive psychology framework. But in that moment of darkness and confusion, it isn't the answer until you start climbing out of the deep, dark hole. It can keep you out of the hole, but it can't always get you out. Sometimes other things need to come first. Sometimes it is even necessary to first take a look at Maslow's Hierarchy of Needs. Sometimes it is sleep. Sometimes it is a good cry first. Sometimes medication is needed first. Once you are ready, positivity is so very important and builds better neural pathways in the brain.

Nine years ago, I despised those chipper little dickens. Today, I love them again. My Pinterest boards are filled with those gloriously, glittering, magical, soul-quenching happy notes.

<u>Sleep</u>

Sleep really is so important. I can't stress it enough. I recall being in college and working two jobs and barely sleeping. I came home one day and got a plate out of the cabinet and orange juice out of the fridge…staring for a minute figuring out what was wrong with that picture… Wow, I needed sleep.

There were things I tried from all the research, my training in college, what docs said…that did NOT work. I heard this so many times and recited it in the Childbirth Classes I taught: Sleep When Your Baby Sleeps - sounds so beautiful. Except, I don't normally nap. I can't fall asleep that quickly and it was literally the only time I could get anything else accomplished. Sleeping at night was more beneficial. It wasn't enough for a while, but it was temporary and sleeping at night came eventually. Again, me personally. You might be an excellent napper, in which, I admire you and might be slightly jelly.

Nap or all night. Whatever works for you. Bottom line, sleep is essential. If you are struggling, you can talk to your doctor about prescribing a sleep-aid.
There are some non-habit forming ones. If you are breastfeeding, talk to a doctor savvy with medication and breastmilk.

Sleepy time tips:

- o Try to go to bed the same time every night.

- o Unwind before bed whether it's a hot bath or sipping chamomile tea.

- o Not too much to drink though too close to bed time so you don't have to get up to go to the bathroom.

- o Steer clear of illuminated screens at least an hour before bed.

- o Make your room an oasis, a place in which you sleep, not work.

- o Daily Exercise.

- o Some people can nap in the day, some cannot.
    - ▪ Figure out which one of those people you are.

- o A good mattress.

- o If you find yourself tossing and turning, try getting up, doing something, then returning to bed a little later to go back to sleep.

- o Avoid alcohol before bed. Sure, it can help you relax and maybe fall asleep, but will interrupt your brain waves and keep you from getting good quality sleep.

- o Cut out the caffeine before bed. I can't tell you what time – everyone is different, but for me, not after 5pm.

- o Try Progressive Muscle Relaxation. Lay in bed and go through your entire body relaxing every muscle by squeezing and releasing all while imagining sinking into the bed and tension melting away.

- o Try not to go to bed hungry or too full.

- o Keep room quiet and dark and maintain a cool temperature.

- o If thoughts or to-do lists are running through your mind, write them down to get them out of your head.

- o Long, deep breaths. Try inhaling to the count of 7 and exhaling to the count of 7.

- o Have assistance with nightly baby duty.

Savor Tiny Happy Moments

Sunshine through the window

Softness of petting your pet

First sip of tea or coffee in the morning

Baby Smiles

All the socks exited the dryer with their match

Singing along to your fave song on the radio

Split second moments of gratitude

Receiving snail mail from a friend

Going to the bathroom alone, no interruptions

A warm throw straight from the dryer

Taking a bite of a juicy ripe pear

Unexpected conversations with gorgeous souls

All green lights

Bubble Bath

Holding hands

Feel of cool, refreshing cucumbers on your baggy eyes

Smell of freshly washed linens when you curl up in bed

Barista made a heart on your latte

The beautiful sound of silence

Pretty freshly picked flowers

Scent of your favorite essential oil diffused in your room

Comfort of an oversized hoodie

Sound of Raindrops as you fall asleep

Getting lost in a good book

Perfectly creamy ice cream

Finding money/spare change

Finding a parking spot no problem

What are some tiny happy moments you experienced lately?

____

____

____

____

____

____

____

____

MOMents

Just like savoring any tiny, happy moment in life, MOMents are tiny instants in time during motherhood that warm your soul and tug at your heart strings. Savor these! Prolong them. Stop whatever else you are doing and indulge in this MOMent completely.

That sweet cooing sound you are hearing for the first time. Keep that laundry basket at your hip just a few seconds longer. Let that sound linger. Smile. Breathe in a breath of gratitude. Burn the moment into the mom file in your brain. Then go fling those clothes in the wash and keep running around like an octopus or doing whatever you were about to do. Little Johnny just said his first word. Put down the bottle you're frantically decontaminating; celebrate with him. Try to have him repeat it. Do a happy dance and make him giggle. Go grab your momma journal and write it down. While you were ranting and raving about the mud the dogs just tracked through the house, little, two and a half year old, Sally said, "I love you Mommy." STOP. Screech. Put on the life breaks. Kneel down. "Thank you Sally. Mommy loves you too." Give her a big ol' comforting hug, breathe in that sweetness. Okay, now raise heck again about the dogs and go find the steam vac.

MOMents may sometimes take you by surprise, stop you in your tracks, make your heart flutter, and can be so fleeting and fast. That's why it's important to recognize and relish in them as often as possible. There's a savory sweetness in precious MOMents that make motherhood totally rock.

Cognitive Distortions

What are they? They are negative thought patterns that produce negative feelings. Sometimes we don't even realize that we are doing them and wonder why on earth we are anxious or down. Below is a list of the most common ones we typically discuss and a link is provided for a more extensive list of fifty of them. Take a look and see if you tend to migrate toward any of these thought patterns in your mind. Once you are self-aware of them, you can begin to recognize, stop them, and develop better patterns that help you feel better all around. In order to be able to reframe thoughts to more healthy and positive ones, it is important to first know and identify which ones are creating havoc in your mind.

The first list is available as a free PDF on the positive psychology program website (listed below). In addition, not listed below, Alice Boyes, PhD, lists 50 more common cognitive distortions on Psychology Today, posted on January 17, 2013, if you'd like to check them out:
https://www.psychologytoday.com/us/blog/in-practice/201301/50-common-cognitive-distortions

A List of the Most Common Cognitive Distortions

https://positivepsychologyprogram.com/cognitive-distortions/#common-cognitive-distortions

Beck and Burns are two researchers who have dedicated their careers to learn more about depression, cognitive distortions, and treatment for these conditions. The following eleven distortions come straight from David D. Burns, MD - Feeling Good Handbook (1989).

1. All-or-Nothing Thinking / Polarized Thinking

Also known as "Black-and-White Thinking," this distortion manifests as an inability or unwillingness to see shades of gray. In other words, you see things in terms of extremes – something is either fantastic or awful, you are either perfect or a total failure.

2. Overgeneralization

This sneaky distortion takes one instance or example and generalizes it to an overall pattern. For example, a student may receive a C on one test and conclude that she is stupid and a failure. Overgeneralizing can lead to overly **negative thoughts** about oneself and one's environment based on only one or two experiences.

3. Mental Filter

Similar to overgeneralization, the mental filter distortion focuses on a single negative and excludes all the positive. An example of this distortion is one partner in a **romantic relationship** dwelling on a single negative comment made by the other partner and viewing the relationship as hopelessly lost, while ignoring the years of positive comments and experiences. The mental filter can foster a negative view of everything around you by focusing only on the negative.

4. Disqualifying the Positive

On the flipside, the "Disqualifying the Positive" distortion acknowledges positive experiences but rejects them instead of embracing them. For example, a person who receives a positive review at work might reject the idea that he is a competent employee and attribute the positive review to political correctness or to his boss simply not wanting to talk about his employee's performance problems. This is an especially malignant distortion since it can facilitate the continuance of negative thought patterns even in the face of lots of evidence to the contrary.

5. Jumping to Conclusions – Mind Reading

This "Jumping to Conclusions" distortion manifests as the inaccurate belief that we know what another person is thinking. Of course, it is possible to have an idea of what other people are thinking, but this distortion refers to the negative interpretations that we jump to. Seeing a stranger with an unpleasant expression and jumping to the conclusion that she is thinking something negative about you is an instance of this distortion.

6. Jumping to Conclusions – Fortune Telling

A sister distortion to mind reading, fortune telling refers to the tendency to make conclusions and predictions based on little to no evidence and holding them as gospel truth. One example of fortune-telling is a young, single woman predicting that she will never find love or have a committed and happy relationship based only on the fact that she has not found it yet. There is simply no way for her to know how her life will turn out, but she sees this prediction as fact rather than one of several possible outcomes.

7. Magnification (Catastrophizing) or Minimization
Also known as the "Binocular Trick" for its stealthy skewing of your perspective, this distortion involves exaggerating the importance or meaning of things or minimizing the importance or meaning of things. An athlete who is generally a good player but makes a mistake may magnify the importance of that mistake and believe that he is a terrible teammate, while an athlete who wins a coveted award in her sport may minimize the importance of the award and continue believing that she is only a mediocre player.

8. Emotional Reasoning
This may be one of the most surprising distortions to many readers, and it is also one of the most important to identify and address. The logic behind this distortion is not surprising to most people; rather, it is the realization that virtually all of us have bought into this distortion at one time or another. Emotional reasoning refers to the acceptance of one's emotions as fact. It can be described as "I feel it, therefore it must be true." Of course, we know this isn't a reasonable belief, but it is a common one nonetheless.

9. Should Statements
Another particularly damaging distortion is the tendency to make "should" statements. Should statements are statements that you make to yourself about what you "should" do, what

you "ought" to do, or what you "must" do. They can also be applied to others, imposing a set of expectations that will likely not be met. When we hang on too tightly to our "should" statements about ourselves, the result is often guilt that we cannot live up to them. When we cling to our "should" statements about others, we are generally disappointed by the failure of the others to meet our expectations, leading to anger and resentment.

10. Labeling and Mislabeling

These tendencies are basically extreme forms of overgeneralization, in which we assign judgments of value to ourselves or to others based on one instance or experience. For example, a student who labels herself as "an utter fool" for failing an assignment is engaging in this distortion, as is the waiter who labels a customer "a grumpy old miser" if he fails to thank the waiter for bringing his food.

11. Personalization

As the name implies, this distortion involves taking everything personally or assigning blame to yourself for no logical reason to believe you are to blame. This distortion covers a wide range of situations, from assuming you are the reason a friend did not enjoy the girl's night out because of you, to the more severe examples of believing that you are the cause for every instance of moodiness or irritation in those around you.

A Loving Touch

The importance of touch is well, touching. During an infant's life, we feed our babies and change their diapers. One of the most important things we can also do for them is provide positive and healthy physical touch. When PeriWrinkle has you wondering if you can do this mom thing, you can and here is a low key activity to do with your baby even if your energy isn't up to par.

It starts with being cradled in the womb to **Kangaroo Care** immediately after birth. I worked many years at a hospital that encouraged Kangaroo Care, aka, skin-to-skin contact. We always tell moms what to pack for labor. I would tell the dads to wear or pack a button down shirt so that they too could participate in kangaroo care with their newborn and that no one would think they were Chip or Dale when they were unbuttoning their shirt on the L&D unit. Skin-to-skin contact is not just for moms. I witnessed some beautiful moments of dads bonding with their baby too and especially if mom needed a break or was recovering from a cesarean section. Skin-to-skin helps to regulate an infant's temperature and blood pressure. It promotes healthy brain and sensory development. Greater bonding and less crying. It provides warmth, comfort, safety, and trust. Skin-to-skin is also great during feeding and helps facilitate more effective breastfeeding.

The Touch Institute in Florida has studies on the positive aspects of touch including after Cesarean Sections, with depressed moms, and even for infant massage both from mother and father. In one study, infants who were given a massage by their father before bedtime, for one month, "were more expressive and showed more enjoyment and more warmth during floor-play interactions with their infants," (Field, Escalona, & Hartshorn, 2000).

Infant Massage

I know I like a good massage every now and then. Babies are no different. It is a great way to bond with baby and helps promote better sleep. It promotes and fosters attachment which is ideal for healthy development. I recall my little one being quite the squirmer and so active. She fought sleep because she didn't want to miss out on a moment of life. Trying to change her diaper was a chore. I sometimes felt like I needed a helper or two. One to hold her legs still and one to distract her because she'd be kicking and smiling and trying to roll. I was failing at Diaper 101. However, I started this wonderful thing after her bath in the evening. Infant massage. I would lay her on the bed and after a few times, even as a baby without a fully developed brain, she understood the association. Bath, lay down on a soft bed…and melt. She would lay perfectly still, arms by her side and legs straight down and smile softly. She began to understand that after bath time was this really amazing relaxation time.

To this day, almost ten years later, I am happy she still understands the importance of self-care and relaxation and hope that it is long lasting for her. I took her for her first official massage at age 8 and she loved it. Touch, bonding, and healthy attachment is just a win-win all around.

Support One Another

One of the best moments for me in healing was when I heard another woman say she had been there and knew. I overheard her talking at a birthday event about having experienced postpartum depression years ago and now her kids are both in college. I didn't want to interrupt or impose so I just passively listened from afar and remember the relief I felt. Like not only was there someone else who experienced it, but that she was brave, braver than me to be sharing her story so openly and seemingly comfortably. I appreciated and respected her in that moment.

I was sad she had experienced it at some point too, but I felt like someone out there got it. I always wondered if more women experience it, but don't speak of it. The thought of that made me feel worse. Maybe it made me feel a bit like I wasn't as good as them or even good enough because they "didn't experience it." Yet, many did, they were just hush about it. What I have discovered is that so many women to some degree have encountered PeriWrinkle, even if they aren't talking about it. I, for a little while, was one of those people. For me, I don't think I wanted to even believe or accept it myself. I wasn't quite ready to share it with others.

When women put it out there, it made me feel like I didn't have to feel so much shame and embarrassment. It was okay. This is a thing. It exists. It is real. For goodness sakes, I knew it was a thing. It was my profession. Yet, somehow, when it hit me personally, I needed to know that someone I knew had it, recovered, and could stand in front of me now telling me that it will be okay and truly sympathize. I needed beacons of hope. I saw a guiding light that day from across the room. I aspire that for you also, that I can be your beacon of hope and/or the stories from other women in this book and the women you may encounter in your life.

Let's help other women. Let's help each other.

Short and Sweet Best Tips for Pregnancy and New Motherhood

- Self-Care is essential.
- Slowing down is essential. Not saying yes to every activity. Actually, maybe knock a few things off your to-do list.
- Sleep. No, really!
- Kangaroo Care – dads can snuggle skin-to-skin with baby too. Gives mom a break. Helps foster dad-baby bond.
- Breastfeeding shouldn't be painful. If it is, seek Lactation Consult.
- Mindfulness. Being present. Enjoying the moment verses being worried about what could, would, should need done…
- Keep expectations low. It's okay to not be supermom.
- After the 6 week checkup, resume intercourse when you are ready. You might need lube. Definitely go slow at first.
- Reach out and utilize supports.
- Figure out what works for you. Don't let comparisons put your brain in a twisted funk.
- Bad day does not equal bad mom.
- Phases. Nothing lasts forever. You'll get through it.

- If you've been in the house too long, get out for a bit. Take baby for a stroll. Visit someone. Go to a store. Walk to the mailbox.
- As Marie Forleo sincerely states: "Everything is Figureoutable."
- PeriWrinkle may think it is burying you…but it doesn't know you are a seed. Blossom my friend.
- Breathe. Inhale calmness. Exhale stress.
- Make a Cuppa. Savor the Aroma. Sip and Relax.
- Even as a broken crayon, I could still color.
- Get up. Dress Up. Go Out. Get your Shine On.
- You've got to Nourish to Flourish.
- No Matter how tiny, progress is still progress.
- And as the legendary fish Dory in *"Finding Nemo"* says: "Just keep swimming."

Mental Birth Plan

We talk about what to expect when expecting a baby and make our birth plans and get ready for the physical adjustment:

What position we want to birth in and where.

The medical team we want from doctor to midwife.

If we plan to breastfeed or circumcise.

We meal plan and prep for easy meals after.

But rarely do we plan for the emotional, the mental, and the well-being of our very mind that sustains us from day to day.

What about a self-care plan? Stress Management Techniques? Meditation? Balance? Support network? Safe space when you need a moment to yourself? Sit spot in nature? Lamaze breathing for childbirth and beyond.

What about practicing now? Pre-pregnancy. Pregnant. Postnatal. Forming healthy mental habits.

If you already had your baby, save this info for next pregnancy. If you are pregnant, I hope you'll consider this. If you know any pregnant friends, perhaps you can suggest this.

Roll With It

I fought the feeling of thinking I couldn't be a great mom if I wasn't perfect. If I cried, then I failed as a mom. If I needed a break, then I must suck at motherhood. Absurd, I know. But I was caught in the lies of anxiety and depression at that time.

Perfectionism. High anxiety that I wasn't or wouldn't be a good enough mom, when I absolutely was and still am a great mom. I was caught up in a hail storm of what other people might think. Each hail pellet another thought possibility. It was exacerbated by people sometimes, but I still had to let go of that. For instance, one time while shopping. I had my little one all snug and safe in the front buggy. Facing me. I explained that we were getting just three things at the store and leaving. She of course wanted something else and started crying. I reiterated the three things we were there to get and go. A lady snidely commented, "Well, somebody doesn't love their child." Back then, that was a lightning bolt to my core. It hurt. How dare she? I absolutely love my child. I can't give into her every request at the store. Just because I wasn't buying her what she wanted that day did not in any way equate to my love or lack thereof. It upset me back in the days and I think I probably cried when I got home. Today, I would probably smile and just keep shopping without a million awful thoughts swirling through my head trying to bring me down. Or maybe I'd have a witty, but kind comeback.

I remember being embarrassed by a public tantrum and wanting to hide. Flash forward to just the other month, my daughter loudly passed gas while we were standing in a check-out line at the store. I didn't turn red. I simply said, "Remember that time I took you to the *Poop Cafe* in Canada?" And we laughed and laughed...before I then politely reminded her to use her manners and say "Excuse me."

Parenting is all about learning and growing. Just like your child. You will grow and grow too. You learn to let go and just roll with parenthood. It's not always pretty, it's never perfect, and a lot of times it is downright messy (literally and figuratively). But it is nonetheless beautiful and amazing and rewarding and so totally worth it.

You are Amazing!
No seriously, you are!

Food for Thought: Placenta Encapsulation

When I taught childbirth classes, something that would come up in conversation often was the placenta and what happens to it after birth. Like, should you keep it, plant it, eat it…? Yes, other cultures do this as well. In America, they have developed something known as Placenta Encapsulation which basically is a more sanitary way of steam cleaning it, dehydrating, and turning it into a powder in pill form to ingest orally.

Why, am I talking about this as your stomach might be turning? Well, some say it can help decrease symptoms of postpartum depression. However, this is all still controversial. Do your own research and if you are considering it, find a reputable center near you that will do placenta encapsulation verses just taking a slab of steak home with you and firing up the grill. Some women have reported it works and they've benefited from it. Others are too squeamish to even consider. And still others who fall anywhere in between on that spectrum.

The American Pregnancy Association discuss the following proposed, possible benefits:

- Increased release of the hormone oxytocin, which helps the uterus return to normal size and encourages bonding with the infant

- Increase in CRH, a stress-reducing hormone

- Decrease in post-partum depression levels

- Restoration of iron levels in the blood

- Increase in milk production

http://americanpregnancy.org/first-year-of-life/placental-encapsulation/

Am I Going Crazy? A Simple Self-Assessment

I have some women frantically ask me if they are crazy or psychotic. "Do I have Postpartum Psychosis?"

"What if I am going crazy?"

"What if I hurt my baby even though I don't want to? But random thoughts pop into my mind like dropping my kid. I would never, but why are those thoughts there? They must mean something."

"What if I am losing my mind?"

So many worries. I respond: "You have anxiety." They reply, "What?! That's a thing?" Yes, postpartum anxiety is a thing. Anxiety during pregnancy is a thing. Anxiety is a thing. Postpartum Anxiety can actually be more prevalent than Postpartum Depression. Anxiety and panic might make you think or feel like you are going crazy.

If you are wondering if you have psychosis, then you probably do not. With psychosis, an individual is out of touch with reality and there is less self-awareness. If you are in the middle of a psychotic state, it will be the people around you who are more likely to pick up on it and notice the changes and differences. If you still are not sure about yourself or a loved one, you can and should always seek help from a professional.

<u>Like a Wise Wolf, Assess Your Surroundings</u>

"It's not always your mental health that is the problem; sometimes the situation you are in needs to change."

If you are feeling off, listen to your intuition, follow your instincts, and take a look at everything around you. Sometimes it isn't you or isn't just you. If you can tweak or change anything, even every tiny bit helps. If you need to completely rearrange the whole dang Feng Shui of your life, do that too. Whatever helps you in your healing journey. Take inventory of what needs to go and what can stay. Take a look at these examples and write down if you have others and then problem solve.

- ➢ Toxic Friends
- ➢ Unhealthy and/or Abusive Relationship
- ➢ Too Many Stressors
- ➢ Unwholesome Work Environment
- ➢ Detrimental Habits
- ➢ _________________
- ➢ _________________
- ➢ _________________

***

If you are in a Domestic Violence situation, find a local shelter or call the

(USA) National *Domestic Violence Hotline*

1-800-799-7233

<u>Ditch the Comparisons</u>

I remember thinking, "Why can't I be like other women who make it look so effortless? They are so happy."

I had waited until later in life to have a child. It was a mindful decision. I wanted a baby. She was planned. She was everything to me. Yet, there I was lost in PeriWrinkle and the thoughts continued tumbling: "It's not fair to my daughter to have a mom like me. A mom so worried and not content. Maybe she'd be better off with those moms. Those perfect moms. But I could never let her go. I love her too much." "How are her legs so perfectly smooth and silky in those shorts? My mom legs haven't even been shaved in two weeks."

All comparison does is eat away at your poor little soul when it is already so fragile. It deserves your full attention and focus on you, not them, whoever they are.

Reality Check – those others…they aren't perfect either. When did you put on a façade to look like you had it all together, when really you felt like you were drowning? Who knows how many others do the same? Who cares?

You are you and that is all that matters. You walk in your shoes and yours alone. Your journey is uniquely yours. You deserve your undivided love and affection.

"A flower does not think of competing with the flower next to it.

It just blooms."

~Zen Shin

"Don't compare your life to others.

There's no comparison between the sun and the moon.

They shine when it's their time."

~Anonymous

<u>Helpful Quotes</u>

"One in five people have dandruff.

One in four people have mental health problems.

I've had both."

~Ruby Wax ~

Do not set yourself
on fire
in order to keep
others warm.
~Penny Reid~

Everything is Figureoutable!

~Marie Forleo~

Perfectionism is a self-destructive
and addictive belief system that fuels
this primary thought: If I look
perfect, and do everything perfectly,
I can avoid or minimize the painful
feelings of shame, judgment, and
blame.

~Brene Brown~

Find Your Inner Howl

You
Got
This!

You will emerge from this nightmare like the powerful, beautiful, resilient person that you are. It can be hard to remember this when you feel like a shell of the person you once were, but trust me:

You are capable of overcoming so much more than you think.

~Jen Burch~

Find good
treatment
and cling to
your healthy
social supports

Women glow differently
when they are loved right
and treated properly.
~Anonymous~

"She remembered who she was and the game changed."
~Lalah Delia~

I see you Momma.

We see you.

You are loved.

You are amazing.

You worthy of love and affection.

All that you do, all that you are,

Is always enough.

We see you.

I see you, phenomenal Momma.

We Need More Women to say,

"I've been there and I'm here.

You can talk to me without Judgement."

One Breath at a Time.

One Day at a Time.

It won't always be this hard.

Post-Natal Depression Is an Illness and Not A Reflection of You as a Mother or as a Woman.

mummy-tips.com

"Rest Yer Wee Legs."

Yes, mommas, rest.

In honor of the front cover and a book I enjoy, here are

some quotes from:

Clarissa Pinkola Estés:

Women Who Run With the Wolves: Myths and Stories of

the Wild Woman Archetype

"One of the most calming and powerful actions you

can do to intervene in a stormy world is to stand up and

show your soul. Soul on deck shines like gold in dark times.

The light of the soul throws sparks, can send up flares,

builds signal fires, causes proper matters to catch fire. To display the lantern of soul in shadowy times like these -- to be fierce and to show mercy toward others; both are acts of immense bravery and greatest necessity. Struggling souls catch light from other souls who are fully lit and willing to show it. If you would help to calm the tumult, this is one of the strongest things you can do."

~"Among wolves, no matter how sick, no matter how cornered, no matter how alone, afraid or weakened, the wolf will continue. She will lope, even with a broken leg. She will strenuously outwait, outwit, outrun and outlast whatever is bedeviling her. She will put her all in taking breath after breath. The hallmark of the wild nature is that it goes on."

~"Healthy wolves and healthy women share certain psychic characteristics: keen sensing, playful spirit, and a heightened capacity for devotion. Wolves and women are relational by nature, inquiring, possessed of great endurance and strength."

~ "A healthy woman is much like a wolf: robust, chock-full, strong life force, life-giving, territorially aware, inventive, loyal, roving."

~"Those who do not howl will never find their pack."

~"Wolves and Women have much in common. Both share a wild spirit. Women and Wolves are instinctual creatures, able to sense the unseen. They are loyal, protective of their packs and of their pups. They are wild and beautiful. Both have been hunted and captured. "

These by Unknown Authors:

Once you're quiet enough to hear your intuition, it will speak to you as loud as a wolf howling in the night.

The Wolf has exceptional senses to detect subtle changes in its environment. It reminds us to listen and trust our own inner guidance.

Part IV: Around the World

Chapter 1: Introduction

I saved this section for last. One, because I personally like it. Two, in case it doesn't so much as interest you, you can just skip it. For myself, I was interested in life and perinatal mental health outside of my everyday box. I only made it to three places last year while writing this book, however, I hope to travel to more countries and continue learning and helping women around the world. I wouldn't even mind doing another book someday more solely on the voices of PeriWrinkle women around the world and their personal stories.

I hope you'll find this segment interesting and if nothing else, a tiny mind escape from your current surroundings to live vicariously in another place for just a moment in time.

First up, my first international travel of 2018 – Iceland, from the end of February into March.

Chapter 2: Iceland

Iceland as experienced by Susie

You turned your flirt game on strong.

Tempting, alluring, seductress with your colors dancing in the night sky.

A magical sea of vast bewilderment. Flickering hues of green, purple, pink, yellow, and blue.

Land of Fire and Ice.

Your countless escarpments with cascading water trickling and roaring.

Your glorious blue-green ocean kissing the black sand beach. Always coming back for more, yet never committing, always retreating. An obsessive-compulsive cycle.

Building, crashing, cleansing, receding. A flirtatious ritual with the sand.

For others, humans per se… "Look, but don't touch" warns the ocean, though.

She can't be tied down nor felt. Don't dip your toes and especially don't turn your back on her or she'll swallow you with one curl of her white capped biceps.

Just leave her be, the queen on her throne. Admire her from afar. Fiercely independent she roams.

The entirety of the island country so incalculably photogenic.

Easy on the eyes. You draw me in and satiate my desires.

Still, I can't get enough. My finger barely releasing the trigger. Drive by shooting - Taking photo after photo and in between photos, pausing for mental photographs.

Gazement – pure admiration and awe.

You are breathtaking and magical, Iceland.

Volcanoes, geysers, and steaming lava fields. Natural hot springs. Snowy mountains, icy glaciers, and caves of frozen crystal water. Constant complementary contrasts.

Your winds chillingly invigorate me and your earth passionately warms my soul.

I'll be back for you.

I'm not finished yet.

Like chasing a lover, we all know how that ends.

Iceland, my cold crush.

I dream of a blissful matrimony complete with your Happy Marriage Cake.

With each visit, I know you will always make me blush.

If I could sum up my trip to Iceland in one sentence…well, I can't…so how about three:

1) There's a mystical surprise around every corner.
2) It's just … right over there.
3) Speechless, Breathless, Magical

I did not have my hopes set on seeing the Northern Lights. Did I want to? Absolutely yes! But I had read that some people can go for weeks and not see or go on special tours and still not see them. So, I certainly was not expecting the most amazing surprise at 4:30am in Iceland when the pilot announced we would be descending and oh yeah, by the way, look out your window. THE NORTHERN LIGHTS and I hadn't even landed in Iceland yet. To be in the sky, immersed in such gloriousness, was not only unexpected, but a life experience too great for words. I was counting my blessings and just allowed my body to be completely consumed with feelings of awe, and wonder, and absolute gratitude.

I, of course, visited the well-known Blue Lagoon, but also had to stop at the The Secret Lagoon - Gamla Laugin. A total gem in Fludir and also a part of the Golden Circle. Entering this particular lagoon was a bit magical seeing steam rising from, not just the pool, but the surrounding land. People congregating and relaxing. A mom holding her newborn baby above the water, smiling. A very happy mother and baby. In my eyes I see bonding and attachment. My heart is warmed with the water. Temperature around 40 degrees Celsius/104 degrees Fahrenheit.

I also saw people walking around the pool on wooden path. I wondered why on earth they would want to be roaming in the frigid air in their swimsuits. Curiosity got the best of me though and I had to go explore too. I am so glad I did. I actually enjoyed it so much, that I went for another walk around later. I called it my mindful walk. I followed the *"Yellow Brick Road."* Yes, despite it being a wooden walkway, I may have started singing that to myself when I first took step until I cleared my mind and eased into the beauty around me. The air was brisk and cool. A nice change after getting out of the hot pool. I could hear the earth gurgling and bubbling underneath me and the steam from the warm earth was continually rising in a perfect balanced contrast of hot and cold. Temperature signs of 90-100 degrees Celsius in some watery areas off the path will surely keep you on the path. I paused many times to take in the scenery. A lovely sensation.

Moments where the steam is so dense you feel like you're about to walk into a mystical land and get lost nowhere. Re-emerging and seeing horses out in the field. Then walking through the steamy mist again and emerging to see a geyser. A litli geysir. I had no idea there would be a small, spouting geyser here. Bubbling and erupting. It was a spectacular gem.

This was only a touch of my visit. I also saw the black sand beach and basalt columns. Waterfalls galore. A weather storm interrupted my visit to the diamond beach and ice cave but gives me reason to return.

My point to first describing all this beauty…I wonder, in a country filled with so much wonder, magic, and exquisiteness, it must be a place on earth void of PeriWrinkle, Right?! Wrong. There is literally no-where and no-one that is not vulnerable to it.

Perinatal mood issues hit even Iceland. As bitter as perhaps the Fermented Shark. Yes, I tried it. At Café Loki, across from Hallgrimskirkja church, I tasted Kæstur hákarl…fermented shark. It is usually Greenland or other sleeper shark that is cured and hung to dry. Well…also, decapitated, gutted, buried under rocks and sand for 6-12 weeks and then finally hung to dry. Sound a little like postpartum depression? … I think so. A fermentation process of about 4-6 months. Yes, rotting shark is a local delicacy. See, even good things come from dark places. I digress, but yes, even in Iceland, moods can feel as buried as their sharks and as cold as their storms when it comes to pregnancy and postpartum.

The University of Iceland released a study on the relationship between pregnancy mental health and social support. A strong testament to having a good social support system, healthy relationship and increased romantic attachment.

Like elsewhere in the world, prior depressive episodes and/or depression during pregnancy was also associated with a greater risk factor for postpartum depression. The same was true for anxiety and of those who experienced anxiety symptoms during pregnancy, 64 percent continued to experience anxiety at postpartum. Lack of social support correlates to great risk factors. However, so does relationship quality. Being married has been associated with better mental health (Barett, 200; Lehtinen and Joukamaa, 1994). However, I would have to add that a good, satisfactory, high quality marriage increases overall well-being because another study found that both men and women, who were dissatisfied in their marriages, were almost three times more likely to meet criteria for a major depressive disorder (Whisman and Bruce, 1999).

The study included 2411 participants, all Icelandic women attending prenatal care in 11 Primary Health Care Centers in Iceland. Participants had to be at least 16 years or older and be able to speak and read Icelandic. Measures included

- o The Edinburgh Postnatal Depression Scale (EPDS) (Cox, Holden and Sagorcsky, 1987)
- o The Depression, Anxiety and Stress Scale (DASS) (Lovibond and Lovibond, 1995)
- o The Dyadic Adjustment Scale (DAS) (Spanier, 1976) – for relationship satisfaction.
- o Experiences in Close Relationships (ECR) (Brennan, Clark and Shaver, 1998).
- o The Mini-International Neuropsychiatric Interview Plus (MINI-PLUS)

Some results of the study:

One snag was that besides depression, other common mental disorders in pregnancy have not received much attention. So the percentage of Icelandic women in this study diagnosed with depression was similar to the mean percentage reported in a meta-analysis conducted by Gaynes et al. (2005).

There was evidence that lower educational levels and poor financial status as well as previous or current mental treatment increased the likelihood of women being diagnosed during pregnancy. Other risk factors: unmarried, living alone, and smoking.

An interesting take: there was only a small difference with women diagnosed with common mental disorders having perceived less social support from significant others and family than non-diagnosed women. However, more noticeable was the difference in regards to support from friends. Therefore, support from friends might be particularly of importance too to pregnant women in Iceland. Given that it is a small country and family members tend to live relatively close to one another, support in Iceland might be more common than in other larger countries, but is nonetheless important. (Kristjansdottir).

Besties for the win. Friends, you are important too and can be an essential help to your friends when PeriWrinkle has abducted them.

One last thought on Iceland that I'd like to share more as a recovery tool. I watched a Netflix Documentary: *Innsæi: The Power of Intuition. Innsæi* is an Icelandic concept in regards to humans connecting through empathy and intuition. A powerful, moving, and informative film. It discussed unhappiness because of our disconnection and how to connect with ourselves and others via mind, body, soul and whole brain. There were discussions on taking risks, being out of our comfort zone, benefiting from failure, immersing ourselves in nature, shutting out distractions and noise, mindfulness, attending to our roots and more. I highly recommend watching this whether you are struggling with a mental illness or not. I think it is a wonderful concept for mothers to connect with themselves, their intuition, and thus enhancing their bond with baby. Just being and enjoying instead of rushing or feeling pressured to be perfect or do too much.

Chapter 3: Ireland

It all began with a disagreement between my seven year old daughter and myself. She told me with a country accent: "I'm Irish!" By the twang, I wasn't sure if she really meant Irish, or redneck. I told her she is not. I said, "We're a little Italian and I am not sure what else." We argued several times over this until my dear friend bought me a DNA kit for Christmas and we settled that argument. Total mom fashion.

Turns out…we are Irish. Great Britain first, then Ireland, Italy, Greece, and even a tiny percentage of Russia and West Asia.

She was right. I had been saving for a few years for a trip to Italy, but Ireland came first. I was actually very excited because my daughter has really enjoyed learning about being of Irish decent. She loves dragons and castles and doing the Irish jig. It was fascinating to see her begin to immerse herself in learning more and more and intensifying her desire to travel there. The joy in her heart and the excitement in her eyes opened me up to a new travel location and I couldn't pick a better travel buddy.

On St Patrick's Eve, my daughter set a trap. On St Patrick's Day 2018, the "leprechaun" escaped the trap and left a note: "You scared the poo out of me when you tried to catch me." And yes, there was a swirly pile of poo on the floor – green toothpaste if you're interested. His trail led to her plane tickets and the little bugga left mommy a glittery green mess on the floor and a fake gold coin trail. Her reaction…priceless. I had to make this happen. These moments are what life is all about.

She turned nine the month before the trip. We met with good friends, Matt and Melissa, who had been there a few times to gain knowledge and advice and talked to our friend Gretchen, who had also been there, to increase our excitement.

And now, right after the trip, I want to share a few things with you about the Emerald Island and PeriWrinkle.

First of all, it is beautiful. In our two weeks there, oddly though, they had a drought so we only experienced about 30 minutes of rain one day on the Aran Islands. Despite the drought, it was still so beautiful. Many locals apologized that we weren't seeing their typical lush, green country. I was still in love anyway and had no comparison.

Second, I went alone with my daughter. Can I get a high five and a fist bump and a celebratory clink of champagne glasses? No, but really. Nine years ago when she was born, I never would have seen this in our future. I couldn't see past the pain of worry, fear, and sadness. Thinking I was a wasn't good enough as a mom to becoming a badass mom who just took her kid over the ocean to a place she felt strongly connected to in her sweet little heart and we explored a new country together – our dynamic duo.

Third…lemme tell you a little something about this island nicknamed after a beautiful deep green gemstone…there are no special powers in this gem that ward off perinatal mental illness. Unfortunately. It happens here too. "One in six pregnant women is at risk of depression as Ireland currently has just three perinatal mental health consultants working part-time." (McDonald, 2018).

As far as depression during pregnancy, Veronica O'Keane, professor in Psychiatry at Trinity College Dublin and lead investigator in Well before Birth, states that Ireland's rates are even higher at 16 percent. (*O'Callaghan, 2018*). Noting that percentage is probably not entirely accurate as many cases go left unreported and unacknowledged.

I'm happy to report though that things are changing here too. More screening during pregnancy is being implemented and adding multi-disciplinary perinatal mental health services led by perinatal psychiatrists. This SPMH (specialist perinatal mental health) model of care was implemented last November. It is also recommended that Dublin have a Mother & Baby Unit (MBU) in one of their hospitals. (*O'Callaghan, 2018*).

Around the world, we are recognizing the need for optimal care for pregnant women and mothers who have just given birth.

One of my favorite darling signs along a bench in Ireland had these words: "Rest Yer Wee Legs." Yes, mommas, rest.

Chapter 4: **Punta Cana, Dominican Republic**

Today, I have my shades on and I am lost in beauty under the warm sun. White sand beaches. Turquoise Ocean. Palm trees. Beautifully sun kissed, tanned bodies. An occasional quick rain resulting in breathtaking rainbows over a vast sea of blue. 85 degree weather. Warm rays. Vitamin D. Relaxing. Heavenly. Clear water. The island of Hispaniola on the Dominican Republic side. A little bit of everything all rolled up into one little island half. Semi-desert plains and tropical rainforests. Salt lakes. Forests. Coastal lagoons. Mangroves. Savannas and so much more.

True charm and Island Beauty. PeriWrinkle can't possibly exist here.

But this is only what I see…here…at the resort. A moment in time of luxury catering to tourists. Out there, it is a whole other world. Many places riddled with poverty. A place some of us flock to for a getaway is a home of hardship for others.

More than a third of the people here live on $1.25 or less a day. A day! The average monthly salary is between 3,000 – 6,000 pesos. That equates to about $149-298 US dollars…a month.

If you're wondering if PeriWrinkle exists here in this gorgeous getaway island…it most certainly does.

In a longitudinal study by Zayas et al. on Pregnant Dominicans & Puerto Ricans Prenatal and Postpartum Depression Among Low-Income Dominican & Puerto

Rican Women, low-income postpartum women had rates of depression twice those of middle-income women. (Yonkers et al., 2001). Issues such as single parenthood, lack of a confiding relationship, social and financial difficulties, and unplanned pregnancies were associated with pregnancy and perinatal depression.

Social support has been shown to buffer the effects of negative life events, but is still lacking research with pregnant Latinas.

We know that positive events are predictive of decreased depression levels over time and negative events conversely increase levels. "It is worth noting that pregnancy was overwhelmingly considered a positive event among the Dominican, Puerto Rican, Mexican, and other Latina women in our study." (Zayas et al.) This is a potentially nice start for perception in treatment.

The article encourages the importance of medical staff to increase screening during pregnancy. That women with low or no prenatal care are at greater risk for depression. That factoring in lower social support, financial stress, and life stress will elevate risk of depressive symptoms even more. All in all, can lead to perinatal depression and decrease a woman's capacity to adequately care for herself and infant(s). Depressed mothers tend to hold more punitive childrearing attitudes than do non-depressed mothers and tend to be less responsive, spontaneous, or nurturing with their infants. (Belsky, Crnic, & 372 Hispanic Journal of Behavioral Sciences, 2016).

They also suggest that third-trimester assessment of the number of negative and positive life events experienced during the past year may help identify women at risk for having depressive symptoms persist from late pregnancy into postpartum. (Zayas et al.)

Some have a tradition here known as la cuarentena, quarantine of sorts for approximately 40 days. Evelyn, a 34-year-old Dominican stated, "It's about food, about sex, about rest." Okay, if you're like me, did you just read that and go "Woah! Sex? Really? Like who is having orgasmic sexcapades after childbirth? You can't even have sex for six weeks after. And ouch anyway." I had to put my wandering brain on a leash. It is actually about not having sex during that time and focusing just on you and baby. Healing physically. Bonding with baby. Usually there are female family members to help with chores and it is good for women to accept any offered help. (Tuhus-Dubrow, 2011). La cuarentena is supposed to help decrease postpartum depression, however there are no conclusive studies. It might also depend on the type of help they receive during this time, whether positive or negative.

Chapter 5: <u>United Kingdom</u>

"The UK was one of the first countries in the world to admit mothers and their babies together for the treatment of maternal mental health issues as far back as the 1940s." (Shannon, 2018). Britain has about 20 Mother & Baby Unit (MBU), where mum and baby are admitted together for treatment of maternal mental health issues, thus facilitating bonding.

Great Britain is next on my travel list. I did not make it there before releasing this book, but I did not want to wait until I make it to London someday. It was time to launch this book. So, I reached out online and received a response from Kerry Thomas in Wales who graciously shared her story with me. I am grateful for her beautiful soul giving a voice to experiences that can exacerbate perinatal mental health issues.

After fertility issues, Kerry became pregnant via IVF. To those of you who know the struggle well, you know the blessing too as well as the worries that go along with it. Labor didn't go as expected. It was okay at first until her little one got stuck at 7cm and complications ensued. She ended her back up in the hospital after delivery for sepsis, a blood clot, and infected stiches from the episiotomy.

Traumatic birth. It's not what we expect or want and have no control over it. It can leave women feeling violated, helpless, and devastated. Kerry worked through her PTSD and perinatal depression and now is a voice of hope for other women. An online support group helped her and some of her go to coping skills include:

Writing   Music   A walk   A book   A box set

If you would like to read more details of her story, please visit one of her sites. I am so thankful she shared her story with me.

Kerry you are a strong, amazing, and beautiful woman. My heart aches for the experience you went through, but admiration fills me for the strength you found through it.

https://twitter.com/KTMummy

Mummythomasblog

http://Instagram.com/ktmum01

http://m.huffpost.com/uk/author/kerry-thomas

<u>Part V – Last But Not Least</u>

<u>Resources and Support Around The World</u>

<u>America:</u>

National Suicide Prevention Hotline 1-800-273-TALK (8255).

National Hopeline Network: 1-800-784-2433

APPPAH – Association for Prenatal and Perinatal Psychology & Health.

<u>https://birthpsychology.com/</u>

SAMSA's National Helpline: 1-800-662-HELP (4357)

Substance Abuse and Mental Health Services Administration.

<u>https://www.samhsa.gov/find-help/national-helpline</u>

NAMI - National Alliance on Mental Illness 1-800-950-NAMI (6264)

Crisis Text Line -free 24 hour crisis intervention

via SMS message.

US text 741741

Canada text 686868

…Resources

A Few International Resources

PSI – Postpartum Support International

https://www.postpartum.net

PANDA – Perinatal Anxiety and Depression Australia

https://www.panda.org.au

PANDAS – Postnatal Depression Foundation UK

http://www.pandasfoundation.org.uk/

DONA International – Doula Information

https://www.dona.org

La Leche League International – Breastfeeding support   https://www.llli.org

Maternal Mental Health Alliance, Northern Ireland

https://maternalmentalhealthalliance.org/tag/northern-ireland/

Perinatal Mental Health, Greece

https://www.fainareti.gr/en/

The International *Marcé Society* for Perinatal Mental Health. London, England.

https://marcesociety.com/

…Resources

Additional Websites

Center for Postpartum Health

www.postpartumhealth.com

Husbands and Dads Support

www.postpartumdads.org

Postpartum Education for Parents

http://www.sbpep.org/

www.seeppd.com

www.mind.org.uk/information-support/types-of-mental-health-problems/postnatal-depression-and-perinatal-mental-health/#.XG40l_ZFzSE

www.mothersformothers.co.uk/links.html

<u>Conclusion and Author's Links</u>

✝ **Mommas**: I know this can be hard. You are not alone. Remember that this is only a Wrinkle in Perinatal Time. There is help and there is hope.

✝ **Supporters**: Don't sweep it under a rug and don't leave her alone unless she is asking for a little time and space. It can be a scary place to feel so helpless and hopeless…AND…be alone.

✝ **Partners**: If she needs you and is asking for you to be home, be there. Other things can wait.

✝ There are invaluable resources. Utilize them. If you are not feeling like you, seek out support. Talk with family and friends. Find professionals. Find a support group.

✝ If PeriWrinkle lies and says you're broken or damaged…Stand tall and speak the truth and remind it that you are Growing, Healing, and Worthy of Goodness and Sparkling Moments.

✝ I appreciate you. Thank you for your time and I hope this book has been of some help to you or a loved one.

✝ Many blessing and positive thoughts from me to you.

<u>Author's Links</u>

Books

www.amazon.com/author/susiemolek

Instagram

@octoauthor

@susieiceq

Facebook

https://www.facebook.com/humanoctopus/

https://www.facebook.com/womenandwolves/

<u>Moment of Gratitude – Thanks a Million</u>

<u>Book Cover:</u> A huge thank you to all the people involved to help make the cover come to life:

Photographer: **Rachel Lauren**

Cover Model from Ironwood Wolves: **Logan**

Hair: **Nicole Angotti**

<u>Book Contributions</u>

Doctor Sarah Homitsky – for her writing contribution, her incredible work in this field, and for being an inspiration to me.

Gladys Magazine, Andrea Patrick Forte, the Editor in Chief, and your staff – I can't thank you enough for your endless support and for featuring me in some of your editions, allowing me to spread empowerment to women everywhere and be a part of a beautiful magazine with an inspiring story.

"To strong women: May we know them, be them, and raise them."

<u>Thanks to all the Women and Men Who shared their stories including:</u>

Cindy	Haley	Beth
Lauren	Patricia	Brendan

Kerry from the UK

My Supporters

- ❖ My Daughter, Skyla who is my inspiration every single day and ray of light!
- ❖ My Mom, Janet
- ❖ My brother, Mike
- ❖ Jen and Ginny – coworkers who help me be the woman I am and provide so much support with my career.
- ❖ Terry Kasecamp – she's my inspiration, teacher, and guide in life.
- ❖ Friends, Family, too many to name, but you know who you are. Stacy and Sarah – you rock!
- ❖ My sidekick, Summer – my Bengal cat who sat on my lap or shoulder countless hours while I typed.
- ❖ PSI – Postpartum Support International Conference.
- ❖ Trader's Coffee, McHenry, MD. The team of positive barista's keeping me focused. On occasions I would write there or take home my usual Dirty Spiced Chai Tea Latte and type away.
- ❖ My hometown
- ❖ God and Life Lessons
- ❖ Jason Wu "*Her*" Perfume – but seriously though. I put this on many times when I sat down to write. The jasmine was soothing and became an association for a mindful state of writing.
- ❖ And many other friends, family, and loved ones who have supported me along the way.

I couldn't have done it without you all. I am very blessed.

References

Bass III, Pat F. & Bauer, Nerissa S. (Sep 1, 2018). *Parental postpartum depression: More than "baby blues."* http://www.contemporarypediatrics.com/neonatalperinatology/parental-postpartum-depression-more-baby-blues.

Boggs, Will, MD. (September 13, 2018). *Brexanolone Infusion Rapidly Relieves Postpartum Depression.* https://www.psychcongress.com/news/brexanolone-infusion-rapidly-relieves-postpartum-depression

Beck CT. Predictors of Postpartum Depression: An Update. Nurs Research. 2001 Sep/Oct;50(5):275-285. Dennis CL. Psychosocial and psychological interventions for prevention of postnatal depression: systematic review. BMJ. 2005 July 2;331(7507).

Bennett, Shoshana S. and Pec Indman. (2006). *Beyond the Blues. A Guide to Understanding and Treating Prenatal and Postpartum Depression.* Moodswings Press.

Bergink, Rasgon, Wisner. (December 2016). *Postpartum Psychosis: Madness, Mania, and Melancholia in Motherhood.* https://ajp.psychiatryonline.org/doi/pdf/10.1176/appi.ajp.2016.16040454

Bilodeau, Michelle. (July 6, 2017). *A new supplement to treat the baby blues could ward off postpartum depression. Feeling sad in the days after delivery is all too common. But researchers are working on a supplement that could help new moms feel like themselves again.* https://www.todaysparent.com/pregnancy/pregnancy-health/a-new-supplement-to-treat-the-baby-blues-could-ward-off-postpartum-depression/

Boyes, Alice, PhD. (Jan 17, 2013). *50 Common Cognitive Distortions. A giant list of ubiquitous cognitive distortions.* https://www.psychologytoday.com/us/blog/in-practice/201301/50-common-cognitive-distortions.

Brauser, Deborah. (May 16, 2018). *First Postpartum Depression Therapy Promising in Phase 3 Trails.* American Psychiatric Association (APA) 2018. Abstracts P5-168 and P5-169.

https://www.medscape.com/viewarticle/896699?nlid=122518_4502&src=wnl_dne_180517_mscpedit&uac=38562DX&impID=1634792&faf=1

Cazas, Odile & Glangeaud-Freudenthal, Nine M. (February 2004). *Inserm subrepository. The history of Mother-Baby Units (MBUs) in France and Belgium and of the French version of the Marcé checklist.* Arch Womens Ment Health. Author manuscript; available in PMC 2010 May 27. Published in final edited form as: Arch Womens Ment Health. 2004 Feb; 7(1): 53–58. Published online 2004 Jan 8. doi: 10.1007/s00737-003-0046-0. PMCID: PMC2877089. HALMS: HALMS469286. PMID: 14963733. https://www.ncbi.nlm.nih.gov/pmc/articles/PMC2877089/

Chandra et al., (July 2015). *The establishment of a mother-baby inpatient psychiatry unit in India: Adaptation of a Western model to meet local cultural and resource needs.* https://www.researchgate.net/publication/282905470. Article (PDF Available)☐in☐Indian Journal of Psychiatry 57(3):290. DOI: 10.4103/0019-5545.166621

Costillo, Monica. (May 3, 2018).*The rate of postpartum suicide is high. So why aren't we talking about it? One in five postpartum deaths are caused by suicide.* https://www.thelily.com/the-rate-of-postpartum-suicide-is-high-so-why-arent-we-talking-about-its/

Dahl, Roald, and Joseph Schindelman. (1964). *Charlie and the Chocolate Factory.* New York: A.A. Knopf.

Dye, Lee. (Sept. 1, 2013). *Why do Wolves Howl? Love, Scientists Say.* https://abcnews.go.com/Technology/wolves-howl-love-scientists/story?id=20109765

Eldemire, April, LMFT. (April 27, 2016). *3 Tips for Couples to Stay Connected After Baby.* https://www.gottman.com/blog/3-tips-for-couples-to-stay-connected-after-baby/

Estés, Clarissa Pinkola, PhD. (1992). Women who run with the Wolves: Myths and Stories of the Wild Woman Archetype. New York: Ballantine Books.

Field, Escalona, & Hartshorn. (2000). *Father-infant interactions are enhanced by massage therapy. Early Child Development and Care,* 164, 41-47. https://www6.miami.edu/touch-research/TRIHighRisk.html. Florida – The Touch Institute.

Grigoriadis S, Wilton AS, Kurdayak PA et al. *Perinatal suicide in Ontario, Canada: a 15 year population-based study.* CMAJ 2017; Aug 28;189(34):E1085-1092.

Hale, Thomas W. R.Ph., PhD. (2019). *Hale's Medications & Mothers' Milk. A Manual of Lactational Pharmacology.* Springer Publishing Company. New York, NY.

Katya. (March 2015). *Wolf Animal Mothers – An Excellent Role Model of Motherhood. http://motherhoodinpointoffact.com/wolf-animal-mothers/* The site is created by my company, 27RedX, founded in March 2015.

Kendig et al., (2018 May 17). *Consensus Bundle on Maternal Mental Health. Perinatal Depression and Anxiety.* Published in final edited form as:

Obstet Gynecol. 2017 Mar; 129(3): 422–430.

doi: [10.1097/AOG.0000000000001902]
https://www.ncbi.nlm.nih.gov/pmc/articles/PMC5957550/

Kristjánsdóttir, Sara Ósk. (Febrúar 2014). *The Relationship Between Women's Mental Health During Pregnancy and Social Support, Relationship Quality, Attachment and Compliance.* Sálfræðideild Heilbrigðisvísindasvið Háskóla Íslands Ritgerð þessi er lokaverkefni til BS gráðu í sálfræði og er óheimilt að afrita ritgerðina á nokkurn hátt nema með leyfi rétthafa. © Sara Ósk Kristjánsdóttir, 2014. Prentun: Háskólaprent Reykjavík, Ísland 2014. Lokaverkefni til BS-gráðu í sálfræði Leiðbeinendur: Urður Njarðvík og Linda Bára Lýðsdóttir.
https://skemman.is/bitstream/1946/17284/1/Lokaritgerð%20Sara.pdf

Kübler-Ross, E., & Kessler, D. (2005). *On grief and grieving: Finding the meaning of grief through the five stages of loss*. New York; Toronto: Scribner.

McDonald, Leah. (January 6, 2018). *One in six pregnant women is at risk of depression as Ireland currently has just three perinatal mental health consultants working part-time. Last month the HSE launched a new care model for women with mental health issues while they're expecting and during the first year of the newborn's life.* https://www.thesun.ie/news/2012079/one-in-six-pregnant-women-is-at-risk-of-depression-as-ireland-currently-has-just-three-perinatal-mental-health-consultants-working-part-time/

Mlynek, Alex. (November 26, 2015). *"Ever heard of postpartum euphoria?"* Todaysparent.com.

Nonacs, Ruta, MD PhD. (June 11th, 2018). *Brexanolone: A New Drug for Postpartum Depression.* By MGH Center for Women's Mental Health. https://womensmentalhealth.org/posts/brexanolone_new_drug_postpartum_d epression/.

O'Callaghan, Helen. *(May 18, 2018). Growing concern: Why it's critical to speak up if pregnancy brings you down.* https://www.irishexaminer.com/breakingnews/lifestyle/healthandlife/growin g-concern-why-its-critical-to-speak-up-if-pregnancy-brings-you-down-843468.html

O'Malley, Katie. (February 11, 2017). *Kate Middleton Takes More Serious Role by Hosting Round Table Discussion About Maternal Mental Health. The Dutchess is taking action on raising awareness of maternal mental health.* https://www.elle.com/uk/life-and-culture/culture/news/a39697/kate-middleton-hosts-round-table-discussion-maternal-mental-health/

Rope, Kate. *EXPERTS RECOMMEND UNIVERSAL SCREENING FOR POSTPARTUM DEPRESSION.* https://www.seleni.org/advice-support/2018/3/16/new-study-reveals-disturbing-ppd-statistics

Rosen, Margery D & Diana Kelly. (2018). *"Science Says Men Suffer from Postpartum Depression, Too."* www.parents.com.

Shannon, June. (January 29, 2018). *Pregnancy is when a woman's mental health can be most at risk. Suicide in pregnancy or after childbirth is rare in Ireland, but it does happen.* The Irish Times. https://www.irishtimes.com/life-and-style/health-family/pregnancy-is-when-a-woman-s-mental-health-can-be-most-at-risk-1.3365647

Stephenson et al., (May 2018). Mother and Baby Units matter: improved outcomes for both. BJPsych Open. 2018 May; 4(3): 119–125. Published online 2018 Apr 19. doi: 10.1192/bjo.2018.7. PMCID: PMC6020269. PMID: 29971155. https://www.ncbi.nlm.nih.gov/pmc/articles/PMC6020269/

Thomas, Kerry. *The Worst And Happiest Day Of My Life.*

https://mummythomas.blog/2017/08/27/the-worst-and-happiest-day-of-my-life/?fbclid=IwAR2pD6tPdIMt5tysAZFW_MsUDRfuwENHUBacv_Hcv70jCbqv4ik8N9r5eYE. Wales.

Torrance, Luke. (December 18, 2018). *AHN Opens Alexis Joy D'Achille Center for postpartum depression.* https://www.bizjournals.com/pittsburgh/news/2018/12/18/ahn-opens-alexis-joy-dachille-center-for.html. Digital Producer, Pittsburgh Business Times.

Tucker, Miriam E. (November 05, 2018). *FDA Panel Backs Novel Treatment for Postpartum Depression.*

https://www.medscape.com/viewarticle/904356?fbclid=IwAR0syE7GFo1B

OhM8q0pc3cJ7ro_XKApnOFyXOGskeYyDCBuKHolYWTqgXlQ

Tuhus-Dubrow, Rebecca. (APRIL 11, 2011). *Why Won't This New Mom Wash Her Hair? The fascinating postpartum customs of women from around the world.* https://slate.com/human-interest/2011/04/new-mom-traditions-from-around-the-world-cuarentena-and-doing-the-month.html

Zayas et al. (August 2003). *Hispanic Journal of Behavioral Sciences / Pregnant Dominicans & Puerto Ricans Prenatal and Postpartum Depression Among Low-Income Dominican and Puerto Rican Women.* 10.1177/0739986303256914 ARTICLE. Hispanic Journal of Behavioral Sciences, Vol. 25 No. 3, August 2003 370-385 DOI: 10.1177/0739986303256914 © 2003 Sage Publications. http://citeseerx.ist.psu.edu/viewdoc/download?doi=10.1.1.919.1589&rep=rep1&type=pdf

Zagrabbe, Kathryn, MD. (March 6, 2018). *Perinatal Suicide: Highest Risk Occurs at 9 to 12 Months Postpartum.* MGH Center for Women's Mental Health. https://womensmentalhealth.org/posts/perinatal-suicide-highest-risk-occurs-at-9-to-12-months-postpartum/

Websites

maternalocd.org

PSI – Postpartum Support International - Postpartumsupport.net

postpartummen.com

https://www.psychcongress.com/news/brexanolone-infusion-rapidly-relieves-postpartum-depression

http://americanpregnancy.org/first-year-of-life/placental-encapsulation/

https://positivepsychologyprogram.com/cognitive-distortions/#common-cognitive-distortions

MOVIES

Stanton, A., Unkrich, L., Walters, G., Lasseter, J., Peterson, B., Reynolds, D., Brooks, A., ... Buena Vista Home Entertainment (Firm),. (2003). *Finding Nemo.*

Netflix Documentary

"Innsaei. The Power of Intuition." [Video file]. June 30, 2016. Directed by *Hrund Gunnsteinsdottir*, Kristín Ólafsdóttir. Klikk Productions. 202 Westbourne Grove London W11 2RH http://klikk.co.uk/project/innsaei-the-sea-within/ Retrieved from http://www.netflix.com https://www.netflix.com/watch/80135273?trackId=13752289&tctx=0%2C0%2Ca8d51d21-85e3-403d-9494-d2f360940c61-11334822%2C%2C. Distributors - Mindjazz Pictures (2016) (Germany). Alive Vertrieb und Marketing (2016) (Germany) (DVD). JAVA Films (2016) (Non-US) (all media). Zeitgeist Films (2016) (USA) (all media).

www.ingramcontent.com/pod-product-compliance
Lightning Source LLC
Chambersburg PA
CBHW031101250726

48655CB00004B/1536